Depression Diaries

This book
Printed in the United States of America.

ISBN-13: 978-1537421421
ISBN-10: 1537421425

To contact author:
pjmcardle1@me.com

This book is dedicated to my Daughter Ryann and
Wife To-Ree Nee.
And to my Mother who always had a book in her
but never got around to writing it.
And to my Dad, Bill McArdle who once told me he
wished he could just travel and be a photographer.
Like my Mom he never got around to it.

I'm doing it now for both of them.

Forward

This book started as a diary to help me deal with depression. It seems more difficult to handle the older I get. In February 2016, a few weeks after my 62nd birthday, I experienced what used to be called a nervous breakdown. My wife called it a psychotic break.

It was the scary and horrible. I got help via the Veterans Administration. Within days they did an evaluation. I was prescribed two medications--one for depression, the other for anxiety. I accompanied the medications with a twelve-week VA Cognitive Behavioral Treatment program (CBT.)

For me this has been the pattern with depression. Get an anti-depressant and go to therapy. I fool myself into believing I'm all fixed and after six months or so, I stop taking the medications. Within two years I'm back where I started.

This time, however, was different, due to the psychotic break. After being depressed for more than half my life I finally realized it is not going to disappear. I have to find a way to live with it.

Starting the depression diary along with the CBT has been very helpful.

I decided to document this part of my journey using images of myself created with my home scanner. Most of the images are not pretty or pleasant. After I do a scan, I write about it. The writing and words come from a flow of consciousness or unconsciousness or anger and all the other emotions I carry around.

This is not a polished piece of writing. It's not meant to be. It's a Diary. I did this for myself as a way to move forward. It has proven to be a very helpful tool. It helps me give the depression a voice.

This is not a cure for depression, nor is it a tool for everyone. It is a personal journey and method I use to keep moving forward. I intend to continue using my photography and words to explore and be creative, two things that I find helpful.

Also, I am not a therapist, nor am I an expert on all things related to depression.

Thank you for taking time to look and read through this book.

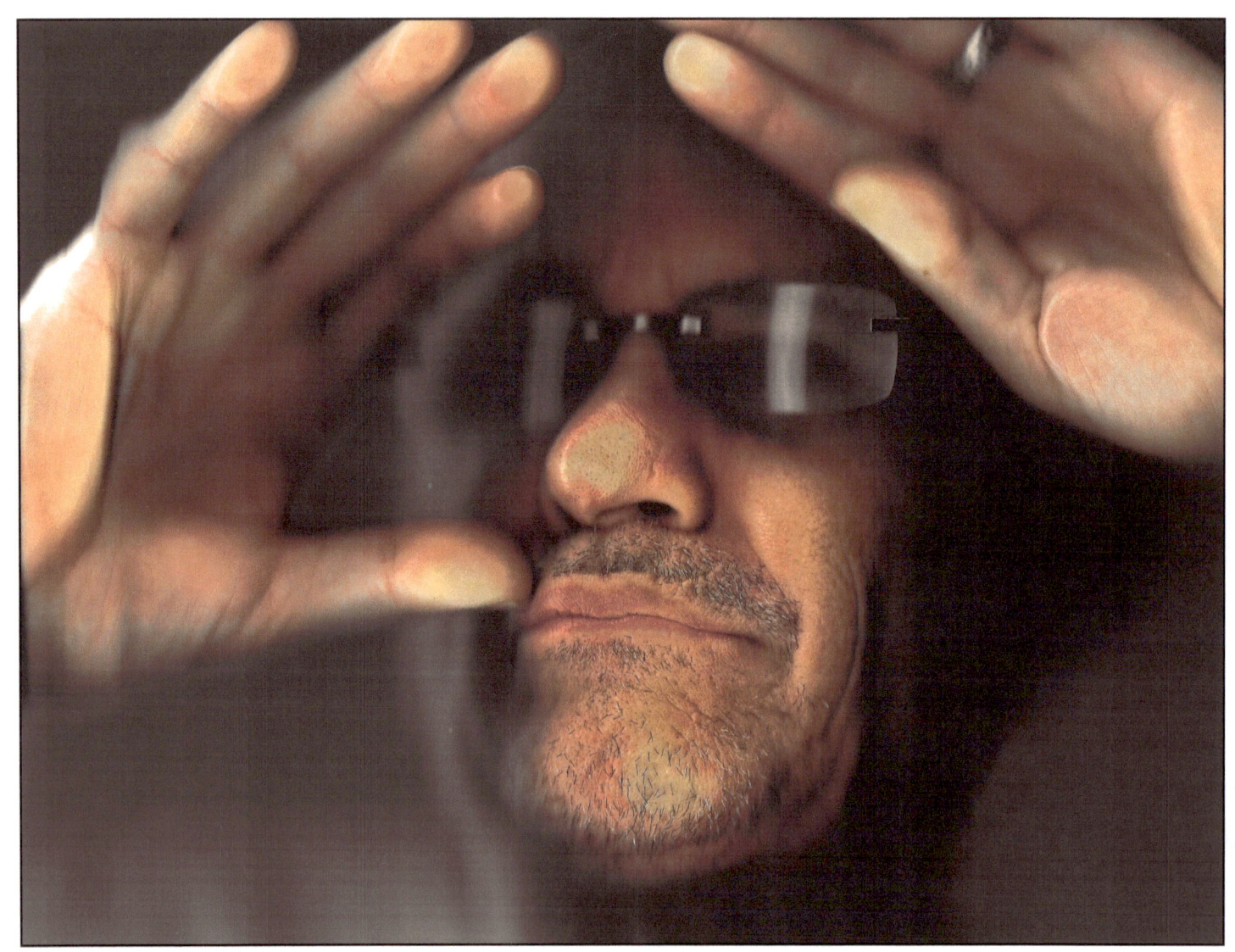

Day One: Facing Depression

Before the first cup of coffee and 12 days into the medication, this is what depression looks like on my face. Twelve days ago I would have not been able to do this. My mind was broken.

Today is a butterfly day, time for change and transformation. Inadvertently or unconsciously I recreated an image of a butterfly I photographed years ago.

It was Photoshopped and I had forgotten about it. A few days ago I found it and thought it was a painting from one of my artist friends. I was surprised and pleased that I created it.

It helped me realize that change is indeed here. And it begins with me, right now.

Twelve days ago I wanted to be dead.

Life is starting to feel good again and I want to keep it moving forward. So this daily ritual has begun. I'll scan my face everyday and write about what is happening. I wish myself luck and am excited about doing this, because 12 days ago I wanted to be dead.

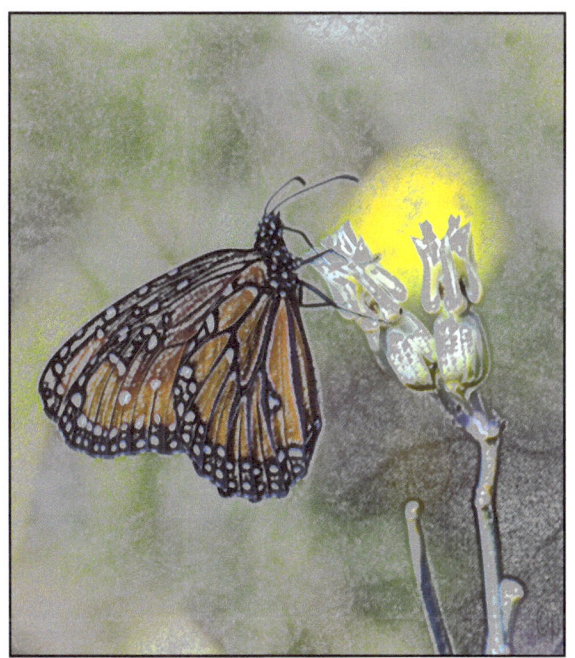

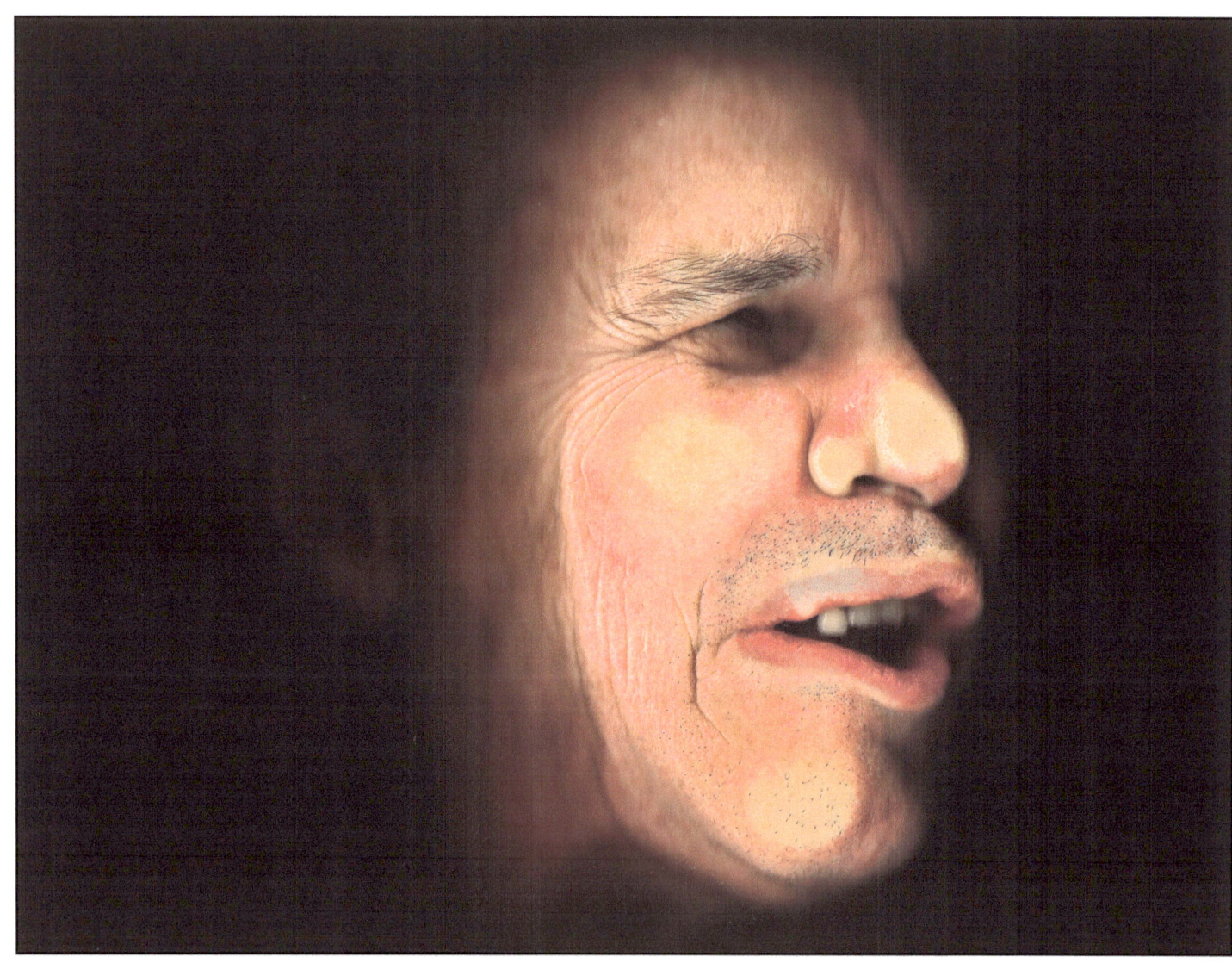

Day Two: Yesterday Feels Far Away

Last night I thought about my motorcycle crash. It happened when I was intoxicated more than 30 years ago. I should have died.

My sister and brother saw me leave the road. It was nighttime. We had left the bar. They wanted to load my Yamaha into Jimmy's pickup. I refused, even though I tried to take off with the bike still chained to the signpost.

They agreed to follow me. The last thing I remember was turning a corner to the long stretch of road on the way home. The next thing I remember is waking up in the hospital paralyzed. Could not move my arms or legs. Very painful.

This image reminds me of that accident. So does the lack of dexterity and stiffness in my left hand, everyday. I was aspiring to be a musician like Dylan or Neil Young. That idea was gone, due to the residual nerve damage. I still walk with a slight limp and get a bit stiff in the cold, but I'm glad and grateful to be alive.

The accident was not the first time I nearly died.

After that my plans changed. I left Michigan and went to Flagstaff, Arizona, and attended college, eventually becoming a photojournalist. Not sure why any of this is relevant and why it is coming up. Maybe I'll talk about it later.

I feel stronger from the whole episode and have no regrets. It feels like it was part of my destiny. The accident was not the first time I nearly died. There were at least two before that. But the accident was the last time I invited death into my life. Perhaps this is why I am fighting to keep from pulling the trigger now.

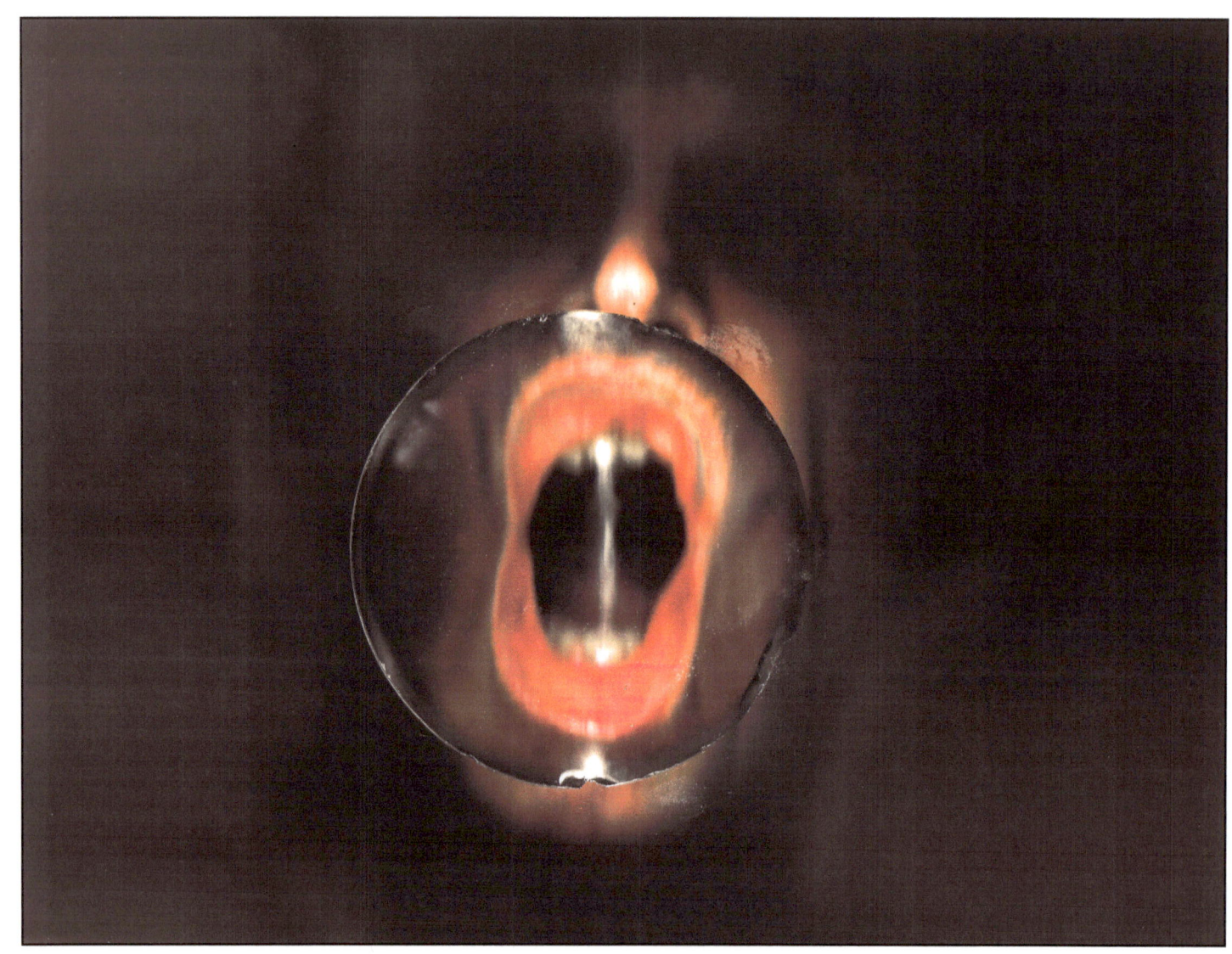

Day Three: Not Yet

I can't talk about this yet.
Even after 54 years.

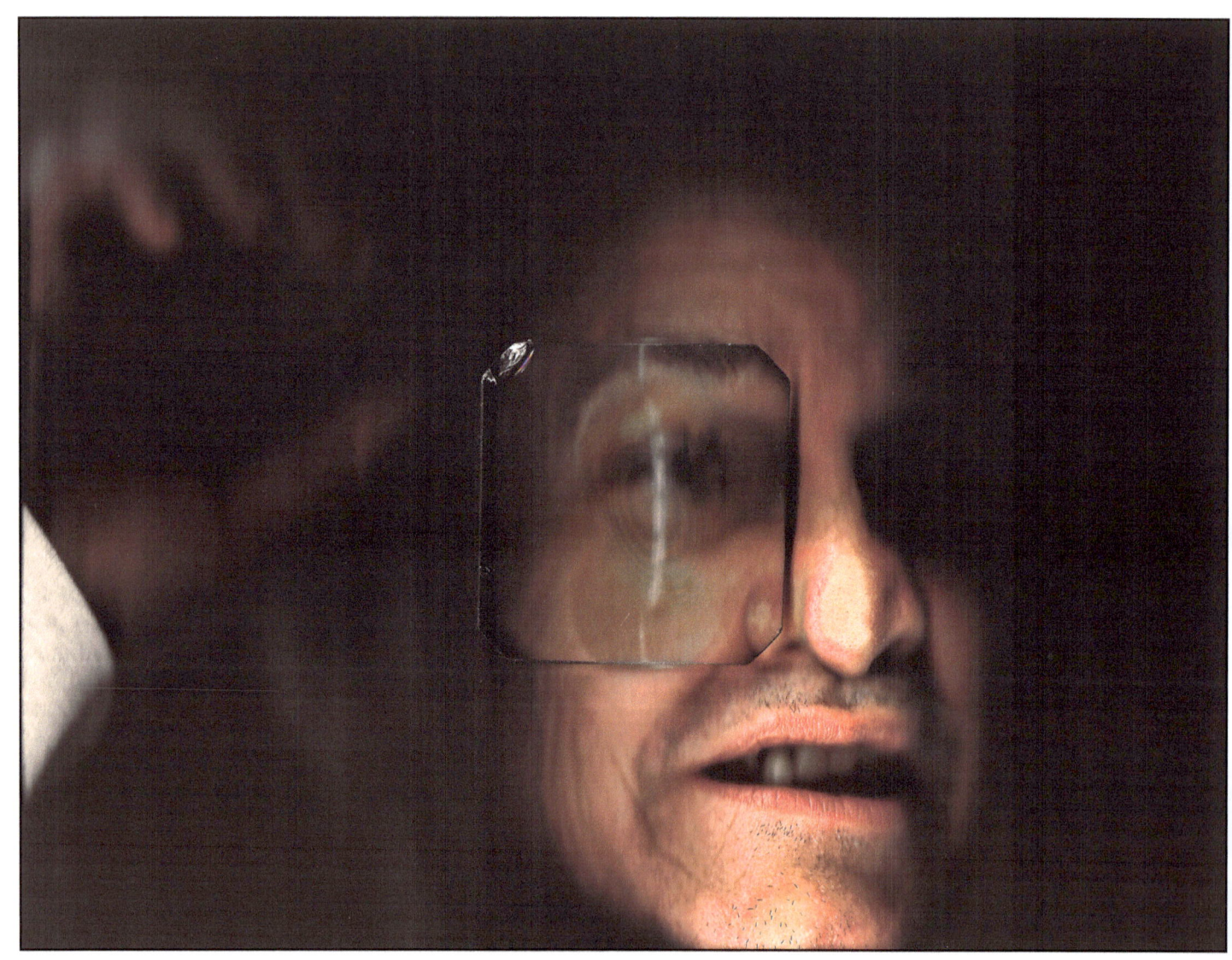

Day Four: Looking Inward

    I have been trying to look at things differently. Or better said, look for different things to look at. I've taken to eating food, early evening especially, outside on the front porch. Kenta, our cat usually joins me. Last night our other cats Tinker and Diamond also came out.

    The Arizona ash tree swings mightily back and forth. The prickly bush which decided to join us two years ago is reaching for the sky. It will be difficult to cut her down. Sad to see any living being die.

    Back inside is Kenta. She jumps on my desk to visit and of course all work has to stop. I'll give her the nightly snack, be right back.

On the porch I hear life from afar. Dogs barking from two or more blocks away, kids screaming and hollering. Can't understand what they say, but the life that is in them I want to enjoy.

    I'm back. It's still raining. Been falling most of the day. Transplanted the red flower into a blue pot. Set it out in the rain.

    We all want to live. I want to live. This is day four. It feels like a long time ago that I started this daily ritual. I suppose it's a gift from the Universe. It seems like time is stretching out. This new lifetime is precious.

    On the porch I hear life from afar. Dogs barking from two or more blocks away, kids screaming and hollering. Can't understand what they say, but the life that is in them I want to enjoy. Like I said, I'm looking for different things to look at.

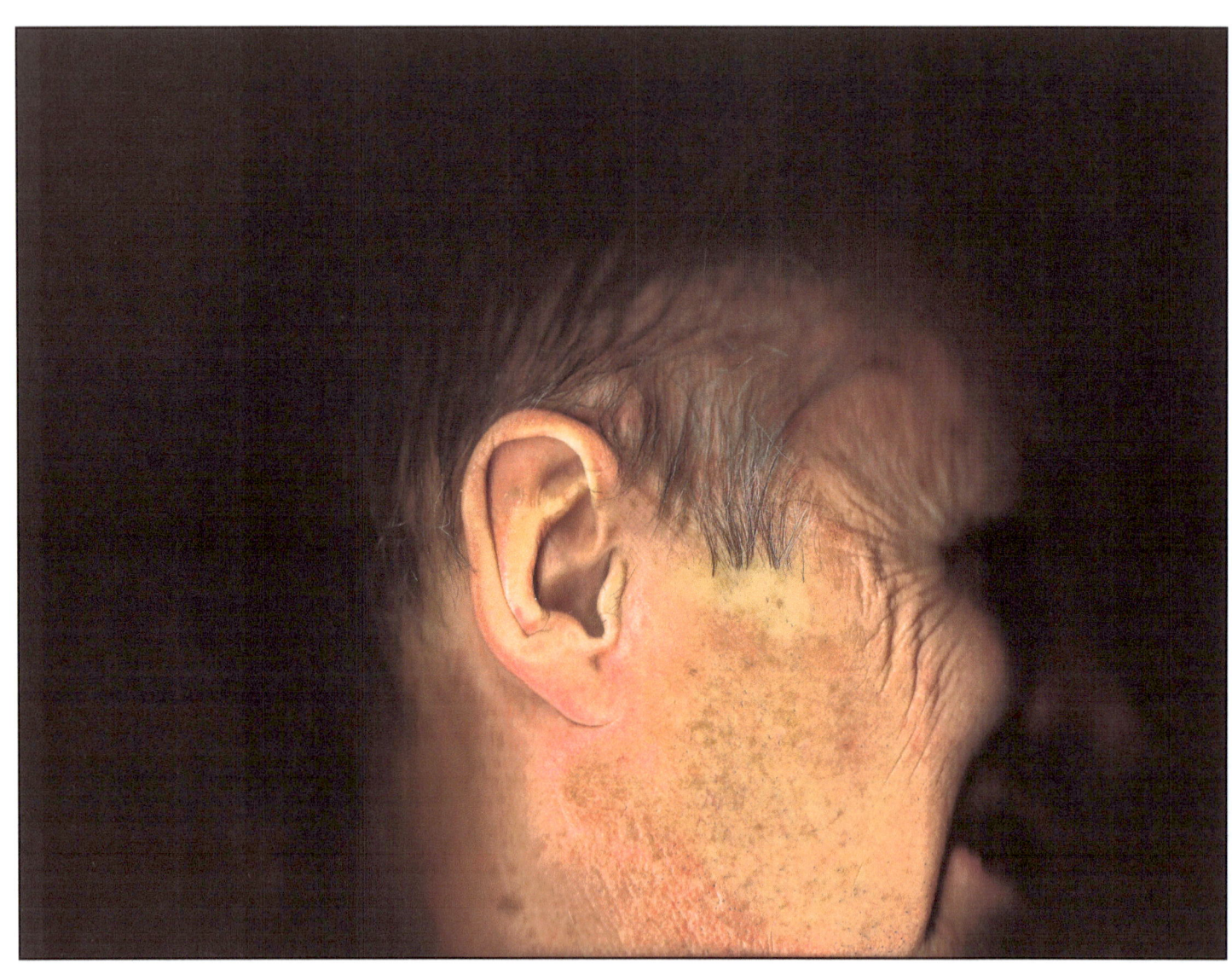

Day Five: Cat Talking

My cat Kenta spoke to me. She is on the desk now, blocking my view. She is a quiet cat, so when she speaks I give her attention and listen.

Not coincidentally at the exact moment she meowed I was staring at the image on the left I just scanned and tried to figure out what it meant. Obviously it means I need to listen.

Sometimes people talk to me and I feel like they are talking at me and I get annoyed and want to run away. I try to be attentive and they probably don't know what I feeling. It's a relief to know they don't know what's going on inside me.

I suppose everyone is relieved about that. Imagine if we could read minds.

It feels like my broken brain is mending itself. I will credit the medication for that.

It seems, however, since I started the depression medication I tend to want to listen and get to know what is going on in people's lives. I feel less inclined to want to get away. I seem to respond more and engage.

I remember how that used to feel. It's coming back. I like it. It feels like my broken brain is mending itself. I will credit the medication for that.

Now Kenta is stretched across my desk, purring and half asleep. Lately she has been spending more time with me. Maybe she knows I'm listening to her more often.

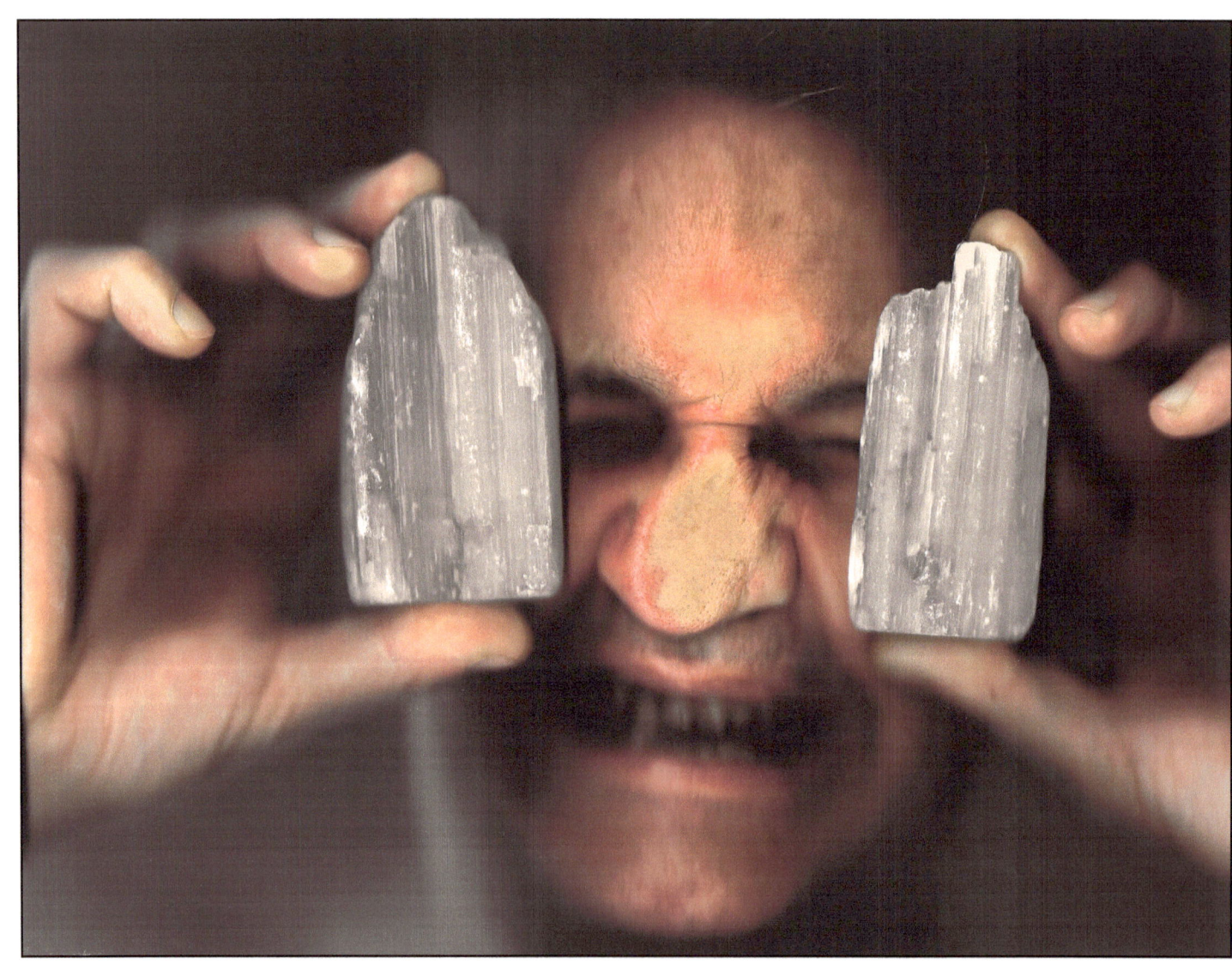

Day Six: Crystal Magic

Last night I had a flying and crying dream. I have been flying in my dreams for decades. Not much crying though. Had a long hard cry last night while flying and dreaming.

 I use crystals as guides. One in each hand as I lay to sleep. Combined with various mantras the nightly ritual quiets my mind. Sleep provides an escape from reality and depression, both of which often go hand in hand. A gift from the universe or a way for the brain to protect us. Imagine not being able to sleep.

Focus on the mind's eye, that spot between the eyes just above the nose. Close my eyes and shut down the outside and inside world. My entire existence is my breath--in, then out, as slow as possible. I feel each breath as it enters my body and immediately ignites and enlivens my entire system.

Sometimes the visions are deeper and various shapes and forms appear. Feels like my mind breaks through and tries to give relief from the pain of life

---

It's like starting a car. Breathe in, feel the joy of life, the sensation of each part of the body coming alive. As my breath comes in, my third eye sees shadows and emerging lights. For me they often come in consistent patterns. It's as if I can see my blood flowing.

Sometimes the visions are deeper and various shapes and forms appear. Feels like my mind breaks through and tries to give relief from the pain of life. Sustaining the feeling is difficult, just seconds. It's worth the effort. Life is good.

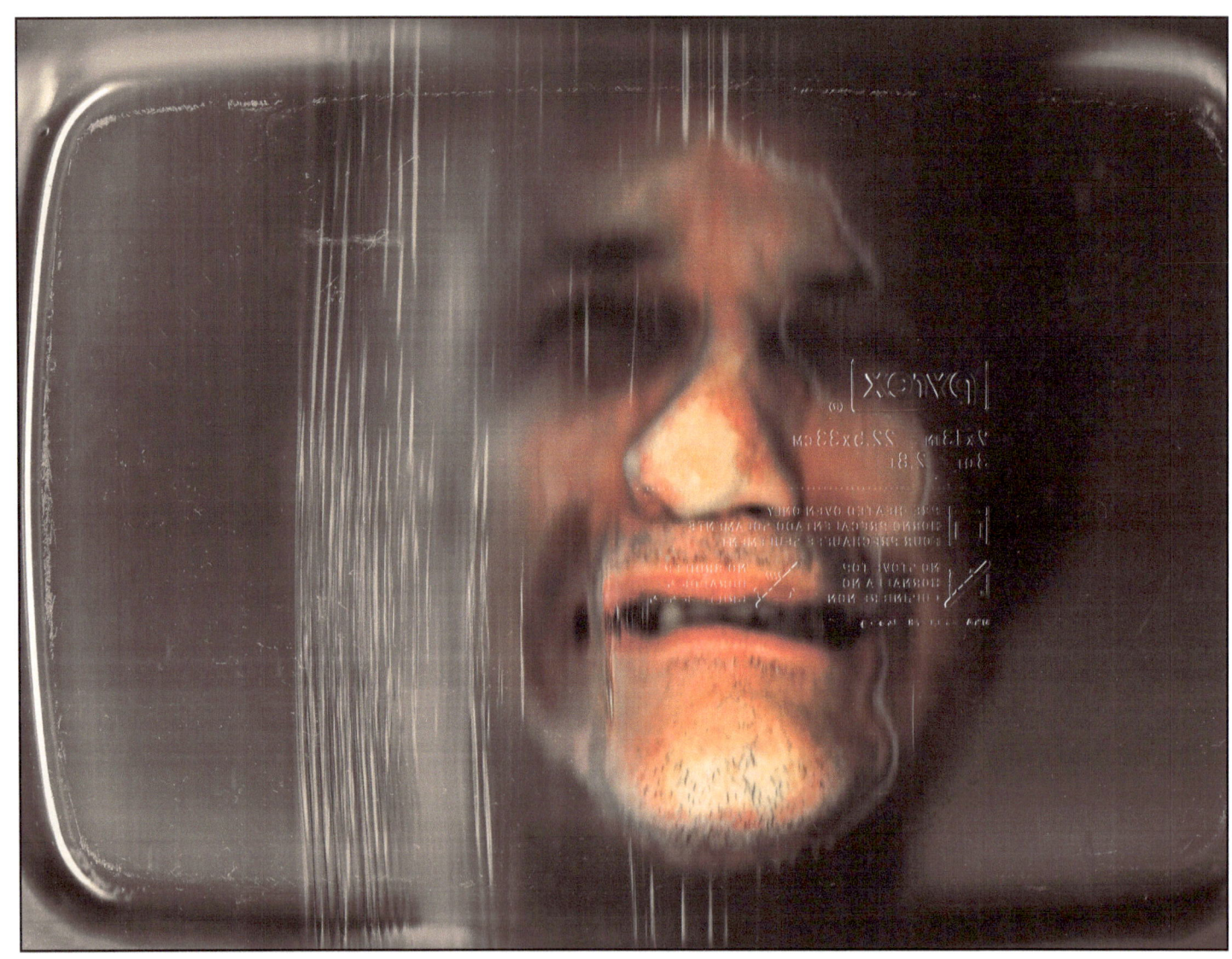

Day Seven: Brain Bake

"She'll twist while you're turning, and shake you while you roll and never, ever let you go. Hurricane got you boy, you're gone, gone. "

Written more than 30 years ago on the beach in Hollywood Florida. The rest of it goes like this.

"I look down at him, the man making straw hats with leaves from the palm trees. He looks back at me and says real soft, real slow... Hurricane got ya boy, you're gone, gone."

And who said "Looking for love in all the wrong places?" And the other one, "Have you heard about the lonesome loser?"

These songs play in my head off and on. These days I'm looking to change the song. I am changing the song. Even better than that, I have changed the song. Gone, gone. All gone.

Death has always been like a mystery guest in my life. If I can be friends with death and learn to live, then there will be peace.

Sitting now stretching seconds into lifetimes, enjoying the possibilities of life. I'm trying realize the power one can wield over one's mind. Just the silent hum from the room coupled with the very low computer noise is blissful.

An occasional car noise and a plane in the distance. If I allow myself space to breathe I can grow. If I stay alive I can enjoy. Death has always been like a mystery guest in my life. If I can be friends with death and learn to live, then there will be peace.

Death does not become me.

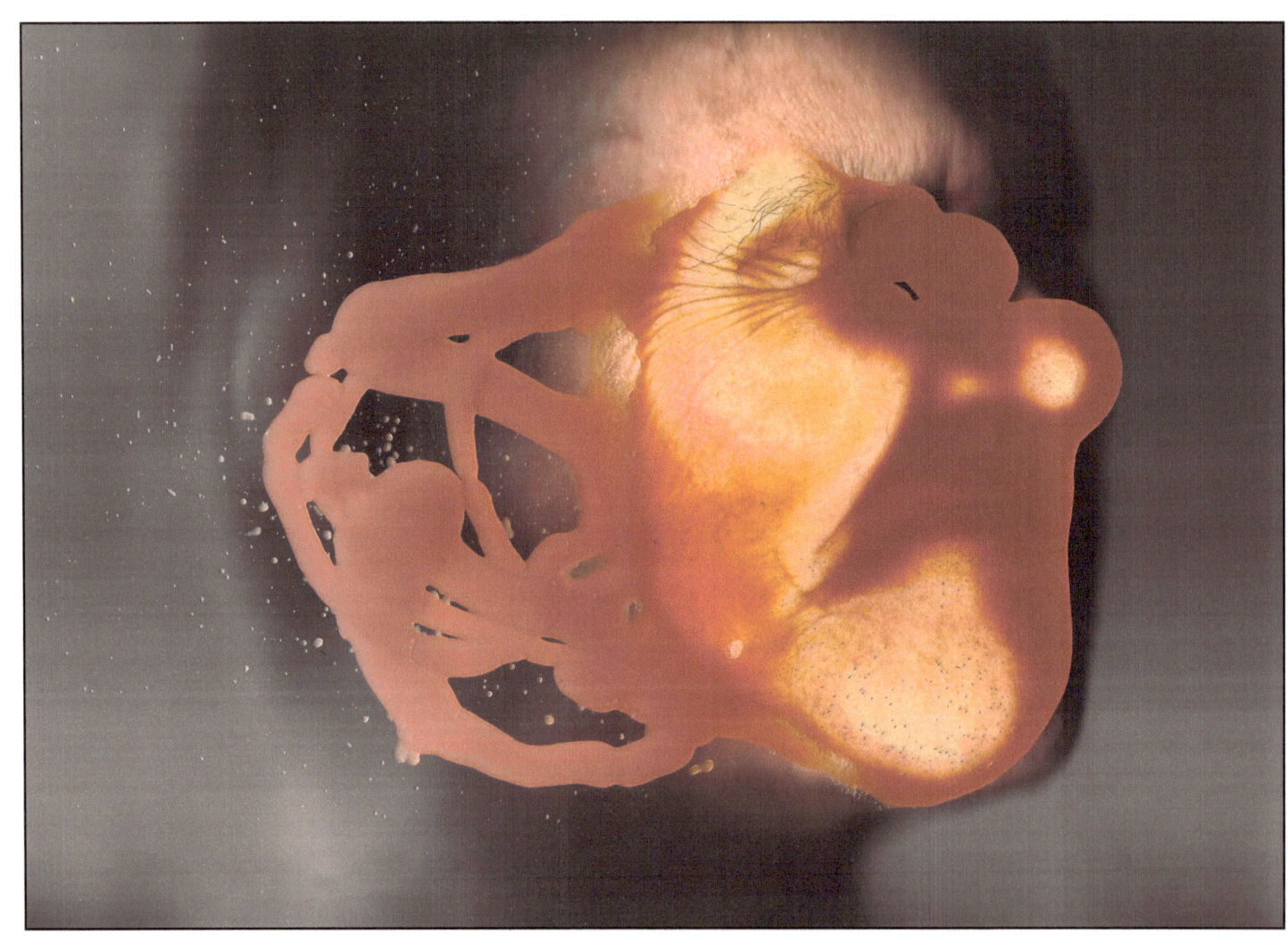

Day Eight: They Shoot Dead Horses, Don't They?

If I do nothing else in life, I am thankful I made it this far. My desire to live outweighs my nanosecond bursts of madness where that little voice says "shoot yourself." A quick glimpse of the pistol being put to my temple. Then an even quicker sense of relief. The pain and agony, the trouble of living and surviving and staying alive is done with.

So killing myself gives me the idea of living in peace. But I'm dead so it's stupid to reason that death will bring me peace. That's probably why I'm still alive, cause I'm smarter than my own mind. Plus there seems to be an intrinsic need to not shoot myself.

Maybe cause I know joy, love and peace in spite of a small part of me that knows otherwise. If I read any of this back right now it would sound silly and rambling and it is silly and rambling, but it's important for me to put it out there.

It's important to give it a voice. I have never given that little killer voice anywhere to express himself. Scary thought. I try to repress the whole idea of putting a gun to my head. I know it would be a disaster and do no good, especially for myself, my family and my friends. And especially my daughter.

I feel like I'm not here right now and this is coming from another place, a very protected and crazy place. It's as if it wants to reach out and finally be heard and dealt with. Maybe I have been here. Have to think about it.

Rambling after Midnight in the past in many different places in other parts of the world. Sounds and feel familiar. Yep. Been here before. I'm feeling a bit dizzy and disoriented. I'm wondering where I'm at and who is talking. I'm wondering if I should start shouting, kicking and screaming.

I always felt like doing that, like going crazy and letting it all go, whatever all is. So I think it's time to let it all out, but in a more quiet way.

So now that I have given the gun-wielding, frustrated thing, person, monster, child in my head a voice, he, it, wants more. See, I was afraid of this. I can point to the images and say, "There ya go. You got what you wanted. See how horrible it really is. See how it looks to others and yourself." Mine. Own it, stop playing, stop blaming, be who you want to be.

So I have to ask you, little crazy person in my head, "What's next? Where do we go from here?"

"I don't hear you, answer me."

Now the crazy says, "You know I never wanted to pull the trigger. I was just offering some relief. If I had wanted to kill, you would have been dead by now."

"Okay let's work it out. We still have a long way to go, don't fool yourself and think it's over just because you wrote some shit and smeared your scanner with catchup and poked your face in it. Oh no silly boy, long road ahead."

If you all want to talk to me or try to help me, ask me first and we can work it out in a calm, rational, realistic and sane way. No more guns to my head, no more temper tantrums.

So if it were up to the crazy in me, I would be doing this according to him or it. I will not accept that. I'm in charge and I will make the decisions. I will determine if I live or die, if I have love, give love receive love. It's all up to me. Everything is up to me.

Who is me, I am me, not the crazy voice or the raging child or the frustrated beings inside me. I am me. I am in control and I am running the show. So here are some new rules.

If you all want to talk to me or try to help me, ask me first and we can work it out in a calm, rational, realistic and sane way. No more guns to my head, no more temper tantrums. No more acting out. Let's all be friends and work on this together until we are all one functioning, happy, adjusted being.

Okay, I feel weakened, The I being me. You others never tire I know. So I'll sign off for now. But remember our agreement, honor it and be nice.

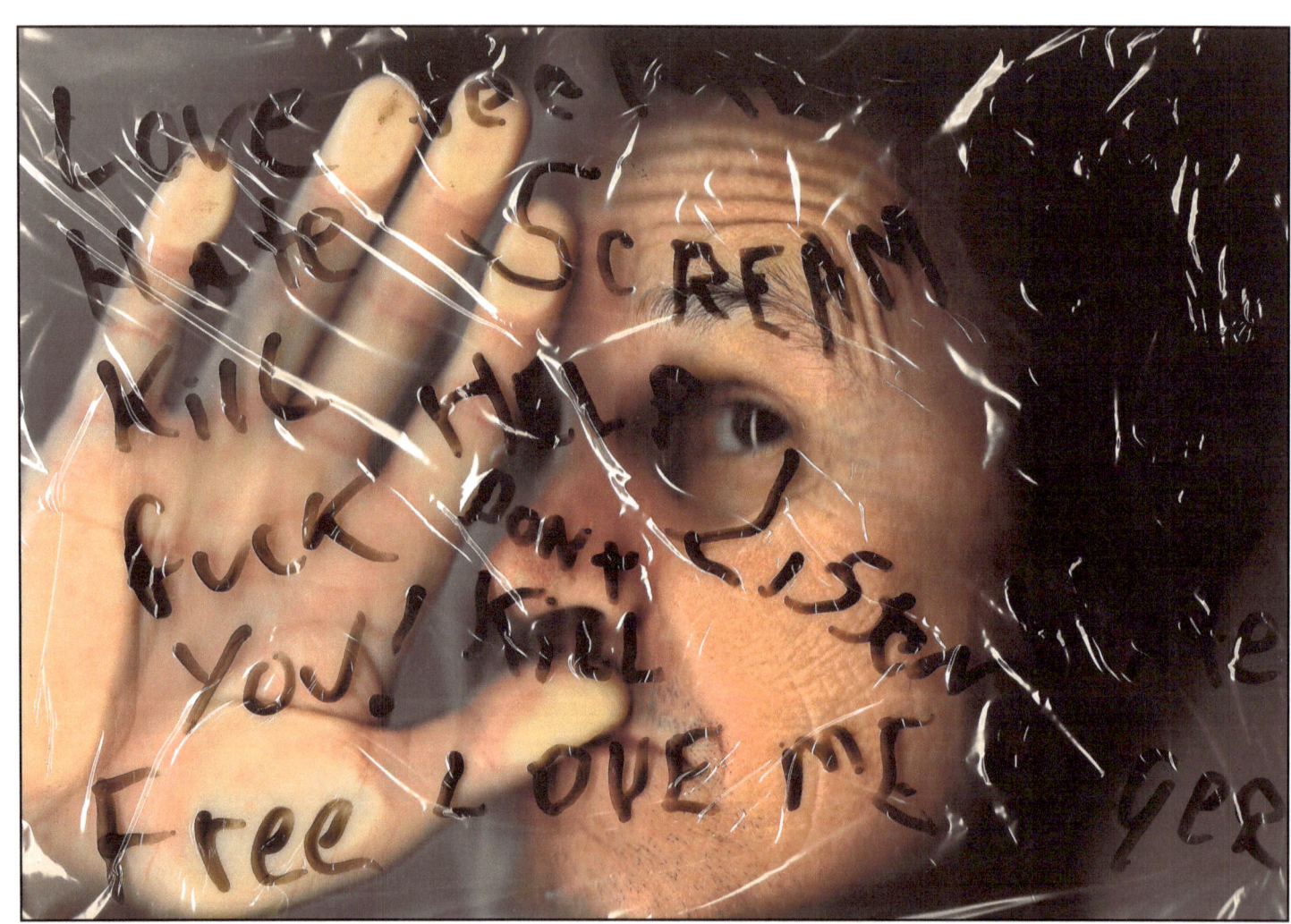

Day Nine: The Inner Child Awakens

How does one deal with inner-child issues.

Kill the child. Drug him away, drink him away, deny him to death. Escape, run, hide, be stupid.

Interesting I asked about inner-child issues and answered about the child, not his issues.

This is extremely difficult. I feel weak, physically as if I could pass out. There are two of me right now. He wants to speak, he wants a voice, he wants love and attention and to be understood.

This is not the first time I have had to confront him nor will it be the last. Perhaps it's not a confrontation, just a love communication. I like that, a love communication, so does he. Just be kind and show and give love. It's as if the child has wisdom behind all that anger. Or maybe the child is split into two parts. One meant to be logical and communicative, the other is meant to act up and be out of control.

"We can eat cookies, watch sunrises and sunsets, talk to people, have friends, have family, make and create stuff and walk and talk without fear. Realize our dreams."

Either way I need to be careful. Coming to this place is exhausting but helpful. It's like getting the truck fixed. It needs a tuneup, so the plugs get replaced. Do the old ones get thrown out? That's up to me. I use them for art. View them, study how they got used and worn out. Appreciate them, but realize they are no longer of any use. They have been reborn.

Probably not much I can do here except to say "I hear you, little Patrick. You are a good boy. I love you very much. It's going to be alright. You are not broken. I'm sorry you had to go through all this for all these years. It's a new day now, we have a new start, a do-over. We can have fun now and enjoy our life together. It feels good. I'm done for now."

"I'll be back. And little Patrick, I will always keep you safe and you will always be my friend and we will always be together in peace, love joy and gratitude."

"We can eat cookies, watch sunrises and sunsets, talk to people, have friends, have family, make and create stuff and walk and talk without fear. Realize our dreams. Work on them without hesitation, keep moving forward. We can be strong together. We can learn how to not be mad together. We have so much yet to do and learn. This is our new day, the start of our do-over. You are a good boy and I love you very much."

"Everyone always loved you but they just did not know how to show it. It's not their fault. Don't blame them or the circumstances. Life happens and we want to live our lives knowing this. We want to live our lives loving others and being loved. We are doing this now and will continue to do so. We are together again and will stay together and live in love and harmony."

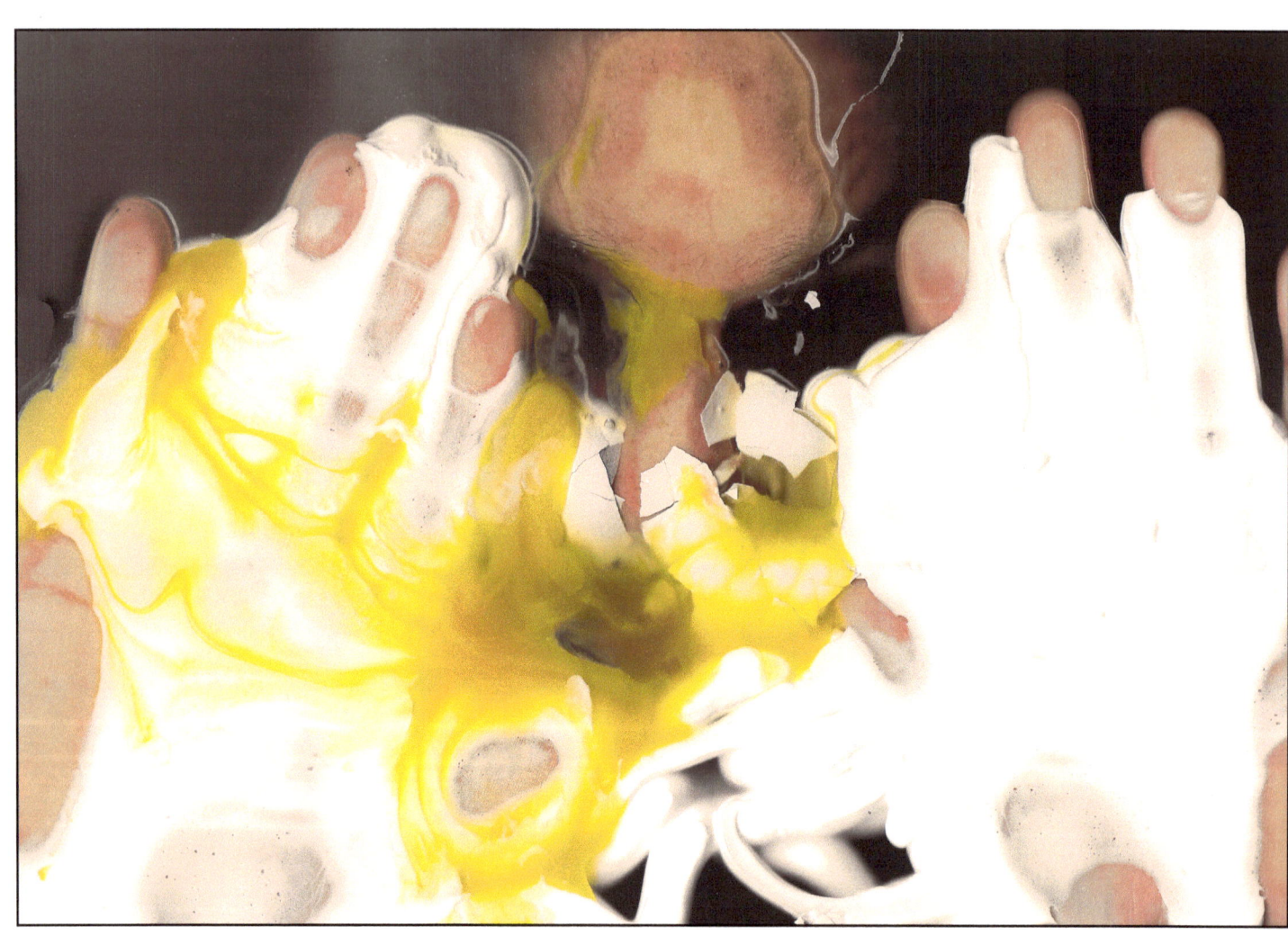

Day Ten: Oh My, What Have We Here

Screaming fist-throwing angry man. Woke up with the thought of death. Just a glimpse of it, a flash across the side of my head. Not as potent as it used to be, but still there.

Quiet surrender, I suppose. Not sure what that means, it just came out.

Sort of stuck right now. Moving forward moving backward a bit. Better said, moving forward getting attacked from the rear. Should not call it an attack. How about resistance or screaming out for help or attention.

Yep, the beings in me still need attention. I now know better. Can't just love them once and expect results. Although it's getting easier to talk and love them like they need to be loved.

Now if I could just be still and always feel like his then everything would be alright. Cause this instant it is just me and resolve. We are doing just fine and feeling really great. One second means a lot when this happens. Stretching seconds into moments then into hours, then days and a life time. How does one do that?

It's like being a drunk-ass fool, but in a sober state of mind. You know the feeling if you drink. The sensation is good, all is fine and wonderful in the world. The utopia of living. This is the result of most drug activity. Hence the reason drug sales are so good and so many are addicted. If one wants to live, however, one should not take the path of least resistance.

So yesterday I went back to driving cab. That was one of the triggers that led to my anxiety attack (which would be called a nervous breakdown in the old days).

And the worse case scenarios happened. I made it through, however, and got a confirmation from a blind woman.

I picked her up at the downtown library. We talked about her dog, blind baseball and other things. She asked me about cab driving. Three weeks ago I would have gone on a tear, telling her how horrible the cab company is and how awful they treated us. Blah, blah, blah, and on and on.

Now I figured if a blind woman in my cab tells me life is good and it is as good as a person tells themselves it is, then I had fucking better listen and believe it.

Now this was the Supreme test. Had I been able to adjust my attitude enough so I could respond in the positive? Had I given the child in me enough reassurance to be able to accept I was in charge?

As I spoke kindly and honestly about my feelings I could feel the raging child. It was as if there were two of us in the cab. A little disconcerting but not insane making.

Ultimately I told her my feelings about cab driving are whatever I decide to make them. She understood completely and said all of us can make that decision and it's not an easy one to make. She noted that we all have challenges, problems and conflicts, but that is life.

Now I figured if a blind woman in my cab tells me life is good and it is as good as a person tells themselves it is, then I had fucking better listen and believe it. And I do and I will.

As my day was winding down I started to see some profit. Then the computer in the cab went down. After a call to support, I was told to take the cab back to the yard. I knew my day was over.

By this time, however, I felt like I was in the divine flow and just did what I had to do to end the day feeling good. I did in fact end the day feeling fine, even though I made $35 for an 8-hour shift. I could say many things here, but I will end with, "Not a bad day."

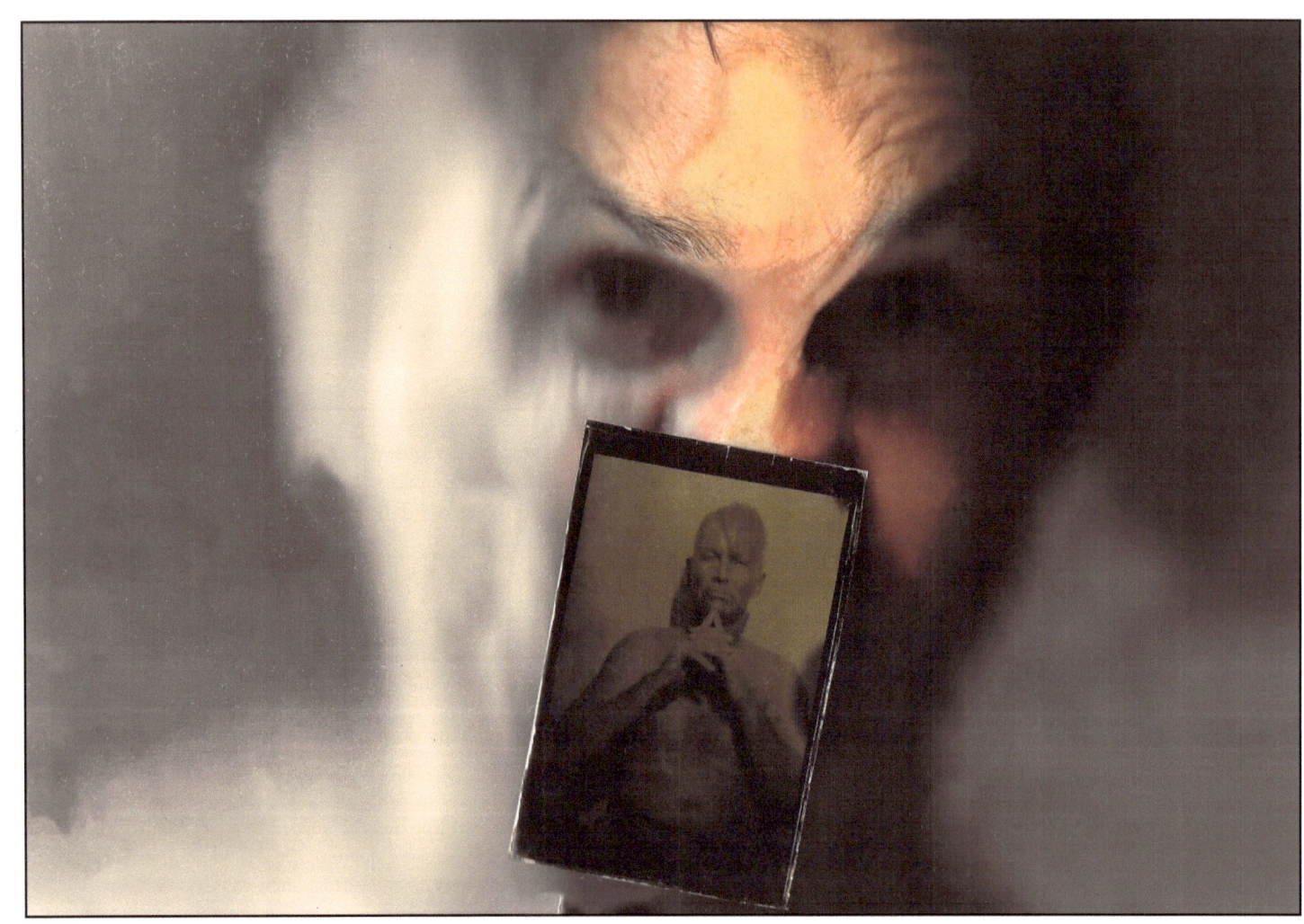

Day Eleven: Inside Me Is Another

So the brain has it's own mind. It's job is to protect us at any cost. The brain has no morals, ethics, love, hate or any other emotion. It only knows how to protect and save us. Of course this is my own opinion and I'm speaking about my own unique brain-child thing. That is why they call it a brain child, cause a child is running the show.

The trigger-happy suicide brain child in me has been revealed. It feels like three people live in me. My inner child and the one I was not too sure about, not quite sure how to label or name it, him, or whatever.

Being here writing and exploring creates a sense of peace and understanding. It gives me strength to go out there, the outer world, the place where people carry on. Sometimes it's too much. Sometimes I want to vomit or scream. Right now, at this instant I feel safe. It feels like I can fix this, like it is being fixed or repaired. It feels good.

This morning the usual flash of death came to me. The idea of shooting myself in the head. It was different this time. I didn't feel a gun and the killer just sort of ran by. It usually stops and points. This time it was just a flash, like a streaker running like hell across the football field.

So if anyone is standing on the outside telling someone who is depressed to get over it , I just say, "Fuck you." It's not a get-over kind of thing.

This is why I have the opinion that this third being is a manifestation from my brain. It's made to protect me. Even if it means encouraging my death. The being pops into my thoughts for a nanosecond. My brain was giving me a break from life, sort of a momentary death so I could feel good.

That little being only comes around in times of trouble when the depression is overwhelming. I realize and know in the deepest part of me suicide is crazy, hurtful and does no one any good, including me, my family, friends, my wife, my daughter.

But I'll tell ya, I can emphasize with folks who do kill themselves. Not the killing part of course, but the idea of leaving this world or escaping the horrible pain of depression. So if anyone is standing on the outside telling someone who is depressed to get over it I just say, "Fuck you." It's not a get-over kind of thing. You don't get over a broken and damaged brain.

It's like a fucking car. Keep it running as best you can until you can afford to rebuild it. And that in my opinion is what can be done to help those with depression. Give them the space, time, resources, love, understanding and encouragement to work it out.

I'm very fortunate that at this point in my life I have all the ingredients to work on my brain, to retool it. I can feel the work pay off. This morning when my brain was trying to save me I could see the shift. The urgency was diminished and the little killer being was almost comical. I understand more about how my system works. It's like a computer and it takes time to understand and repair or reprogram. That's the key word, reprogram, retool the belief system.

I find myself responding to various situations differently than three weeks ago. It's as if my initial response gets shut down because the new programming is getting written in.

It feels good to be in control. If I cast doubt and start being pessimistic, then the old program is still working. Still I have to listen to it cause it is not all bad. There is value in learning from the old ways. One has to be careful though, and try to make the best decision. This is why it is important to slow my life down and give the new program a chance to digest, understand and communicate with the old one. Too much too fast is not good. Just enough is perfect. I'm a just-enough kind of guy right now.

I'm looking forward to the future. I'm very excited to be alive and to be able to love everyone in my life.

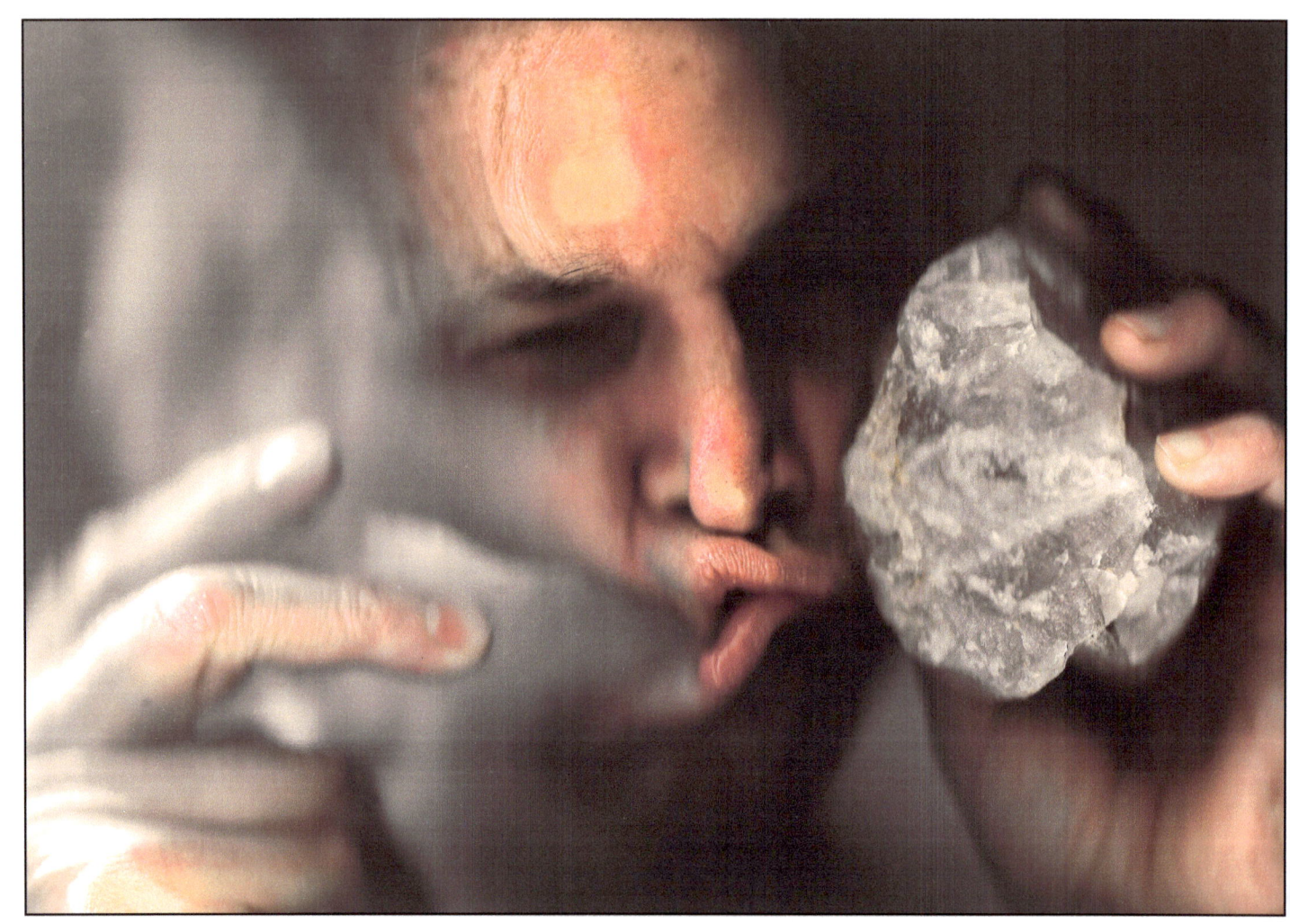

Day Twelve: Jagged Edge

The little killer came back this morning, followed by the rock monsters. The killer was so quick I barely recognized it. The rock monster stayed and lingered and brought friends.

They want me to hurt myself. Specifically stab the crystal, the pointy one, into my arm. It is always the same crystal the same place the same stabbing.

This morning the big pink crystal wanted me to bash myself into my head. Actually it is not the crystal, it is the monster inside me. Or whatever that is. The mind, the mind's eye, that third being I keep referring to. That's who I think it is, the third being/person inside me that was/is created by my brain to protect me, to keep me safe.

How does stabbing or bashing oneself with a crystal keep one safe? There is something else going on here. I need to explore this. It's scary and I'm reluctant to do it. It feels like my brain is trying to trick me into doing it. It feels like if I get started it could get really ugly.

"Standing at the door between leaving and gone." I wrote this a hundred years ago. Feels like I'm at the door now.

 Maybe my brain is forcing this on me as a way to heal myself. Cause my brain knows I'm moving forward and looking for resolve. Maybe this is a way for my brain to address this. I don't know if it is test, don't know if my brain works like that.

"Standing at the door between leaving and gone." I wrote this a hundred years ago. Feels like I'm at the door now. Seeing myself leaning against the door frame, glancing left then right. In no big hurry, just waiting for anything to happen but knowing it's all up to me.

It's my decision. "Standing at the door between leaving and gone."

Well since this is all about resolve something has to move forward. Steps have to be taken. Now that little voice wants me to smash the pink crystal into the computer screen. It feels like the child in me.

As a kid I built model cars from kits. Purchased them from Uhan's variety store on the corner. I had a collection. I wanted them to be built a certain way and it seems like there were not any tools that could have made it happen.

Or I just didn't have the patience or skill. I just wanted it to be the way I wanted. That's what it was all about. I wanted something to go my way. I wanted a sense of control in my own little world.

Most of the time it worked and I felt great knowing I could work on my model car. I would spray paint them, take extra care and keep the glue from sticking everywhere. Then occasionally I would throw a fit and smash the model to pieces before it was complete.

So maybe the crystal monsters are not the third being. I think they are my inner child sensing changes and things are getting out of control. But how is that? I'm moving forward. Okay I get it. I need to reassure my inner child more often and more intently.

Not quite sure how this is going to play out for the rest of the day. I'm feeling all messed up. I really do want to have an amazing day.

Well, I just realized that is up to me. I am in control, not my inner child. So I'm not going to smash myself with anything or smash my computer.

So I say, "Patrick, it's going to be alright. I love you, everyone loves you and wants to be around you and play with you and we do care about you. You are a good boy. We all love you very much so put the rock down."

"So Patrick, let's build this model together. Let's make it good, and cool and groovy and nice and whatever we want it to be. Let's finish it in beauty, love, joy and peace."

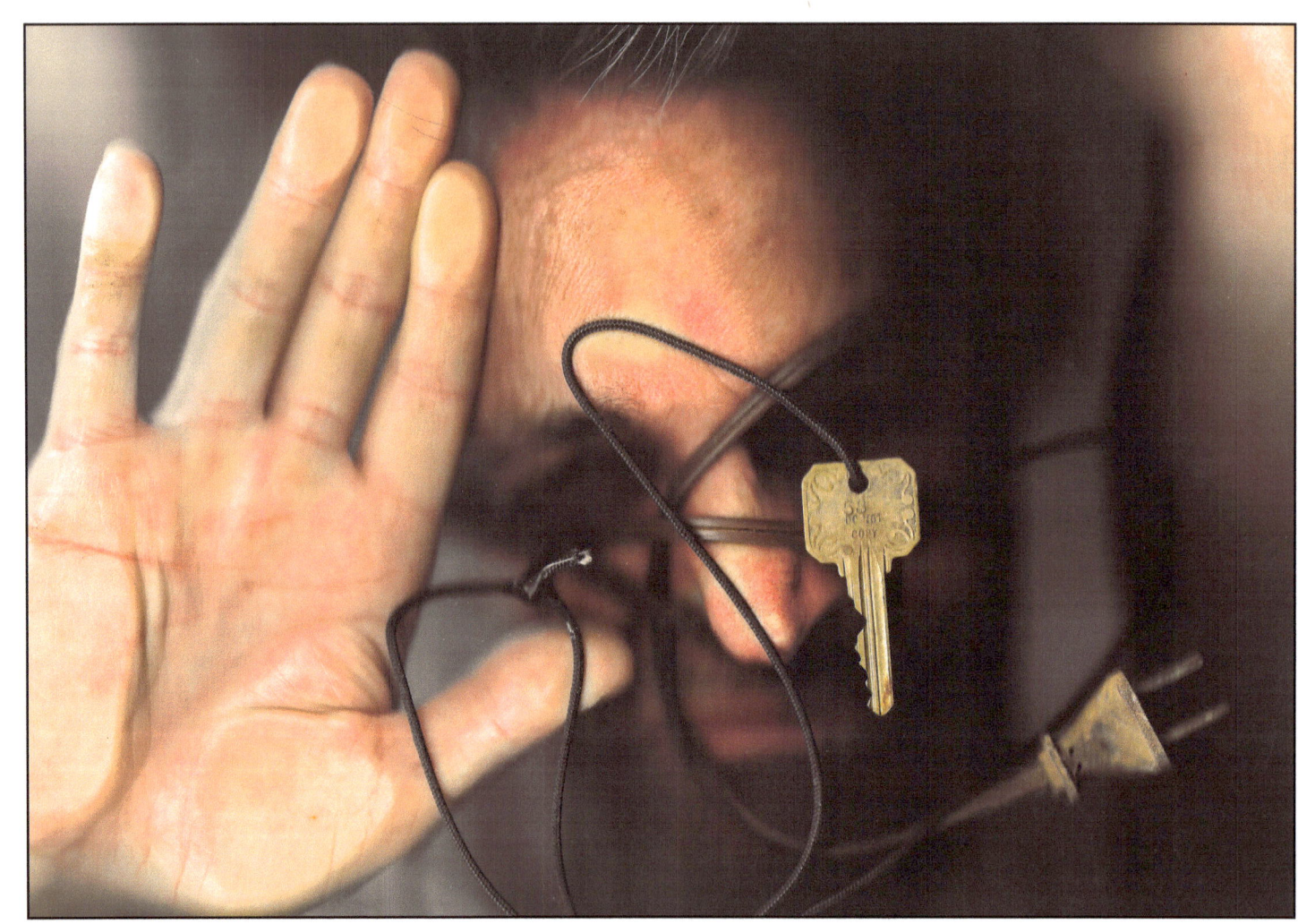

Day Thirteen: The Coyote Trickster

Depression has no rules or regulations. It comes and goes when it wants. It wants to be with me today.

Part of me says "Fuck you." That's the part that wants to be in control.

If it gets out and explodes all over this screen, if it lives on and lives on and lives on and lives on and lives on……..

Slowing down, moving at a snail's pace, all slimy. Scratching my belly to shreds, moving along in the dirt, tearing it up.

Pulling one piece out at a time. One small seemingly indistinguishable piece. Examining, deciding, thinking, killing it, just killing it to pieces. All wrapped up in it. All fucking warped up. Just when ya think it's good, when ya think it's moving on.

Good fucking thought: maybe this is just an act so I can be stupid and foolish. Or maybe this is the part where I can chose what the fuck to believe.

That's the pattern, right. Then we go back to the brain trying to protect the mind, protect me. This depression today, this feeling. Is it a brain trick or the slippery Coyote? Or just life. That in itself is depressing for most people. Not clinically but just normal livable everyday depression.

People always say they are depressed. But perhaps not clinically depressed. So maybe my depression is my badge of courage, or my excuse to behave badly or my excuse for not doing what I'm supposed to do to survive and act responsible.

Good fucking thought, maybe this is just an act so I can be stupid and foolish. Or maybe this is the part where I can chose what the fuck to believe. Maybe this is the reprogramming part that gets sticky and messy and often ends up being the end or going as far as it has gone.

It's up to me. I have the power. I keep forgetting that. I have to remind myself. Yep, it feels like the trickster Coyote is playing and prancing and dancing around in my head.

So let me count backwards here. About 30 days since this journey began. Someone told me it takes 60 days to reprogram the brain.

I can feel some of the programming sticking and hanging in there. It's like creating my gum Arabic prints: one coat at a time. Let it dry, then see how it looks, then apply the next color. Keep at it until I feel it,s done.

I think this is why the gum Arabic printing process is central to me right now. Okay, the program continues but I cannot switch channels.

I'm still feeling depressed. What to do?

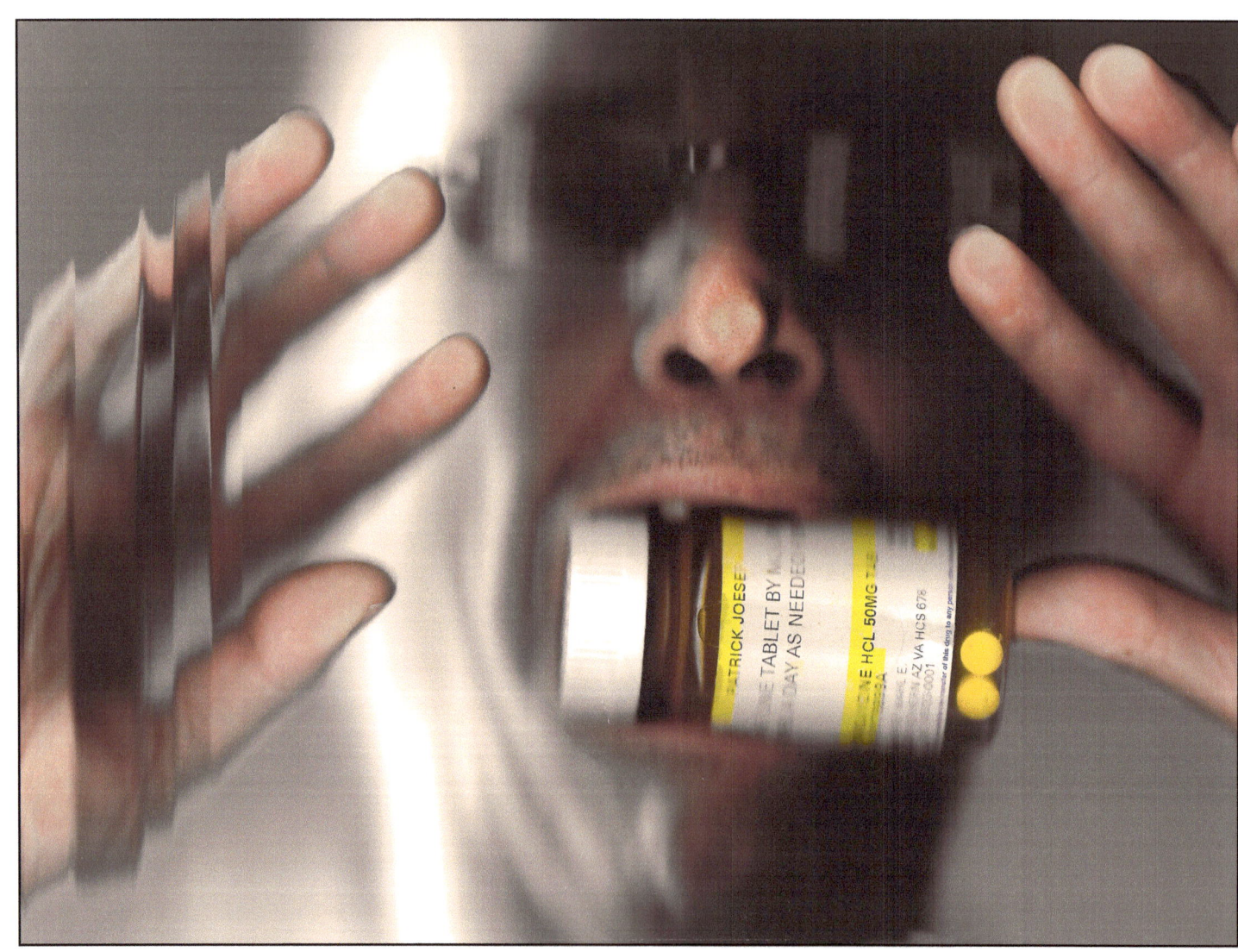

Day Fourteen: Med Head

So my wife says I had a psychotic break.

Definition: A psychotic break occurs when a person experiences an episode of acute primary psychosis, generally for the first time.

Causes: Many things can cause temporary psychosis. Environmental triggers, such as losing a loved one, are known to contribute, as may excessive stress, or the interaction of strong social demands with a preexisting vulnerability of self.

Other causes that have been identified include lack of sleep, fever, brain damage, and even hypnosis.

War/battlefield experience may also trigger a psychotic break. When reality becomes unbearable, the mind temporarily breaks with it.

Parenthood may occasionally set off a psychotic break in men, as may giving birth in women who have previously denied a pregnancy.

Went to the VA, saw the psych doctor and got some medications. The big Prozac and some anxiety pills. Much needed. And so the process began, as can be seen here.

Symptoms of psychotic breaks vary greatly, usually depending on the circumstances of diagnosis or any contributory substance ingested. Symptoms can range from harmless, sometimes unnoticed delusions, to violent outbursts and major depression. The sufferer may also be unable to distinguish reality from fantasy (for example, believing that a dream really happened or experiencing hallucinations that appear to be real). Where a bipolar disorder is involved, crying, grandiosity, insomnia, irritability, and persecutory delusions may all or severally manifest themselves as symptoms.

Yep, it fits. Happened about a week before I started this pictorial journal. Scary shit indeed. Went to the VA, saw the psych doctor and got some medications. The big Prozac and some anxiety pills. Much needed. And so the process began as can be seen here.

Regardless of the medications I still feel depressed. Not as intense, but it's still there. My wife says it's the chemicals, not me. I agree. Chemically, clinically depressed. So I take more chemicals or medications to combat the chemical imbalance. Just don't seem right.

I tried to fight it without the medications. I don't know how and tend to beat myself up. But I'm more forgiving these days. It's the chemical, not me. So I just want to go back to bed and sleep. And I could sleep easily, even though I'm drinking my strong-ass coffee.

But really it's living that is making me tired. I have got to get some things done I hate to do to survive--chores, work, etc. I talked myself into doing this thing today I have been putting it off. Then I got up this morning and didn't do it.

There is always tomorrow. So today I'm looking for a way out, a way to dump the guilt and pain. A roadway to relief. I'm beating myself up. There are these crazy ideas but none with immediate results and I discount them and say they will never work.

Fuck me, trying to balance reality from idealism and escapism is so fucking hard. It's so fucking hard to find a way through. To look at it all and take the reality and separate it from idealism and crazy mind tricks.

Maybe I'll stay awake and keep looking until I find relief or a resolve. It just feels so massive. I'm tired even thinking about thinking about a solution. Thinking twice makes me tired. I'm laughing at myself and at the same time saying "This is not funny."

I feel like a contradiction. Can contradictions be human? It just feels so crazy and insane and out of control and corrupt and evil and mean and deceitful and lopsided and just all fucked up. It's like I jumped into a pool of fuck-up water. It feels like I live in Fuck-Up City.

The medications.. Are they working? What do you think? And who is "you" by the way? Oh fuck, another day in a round fucking world.

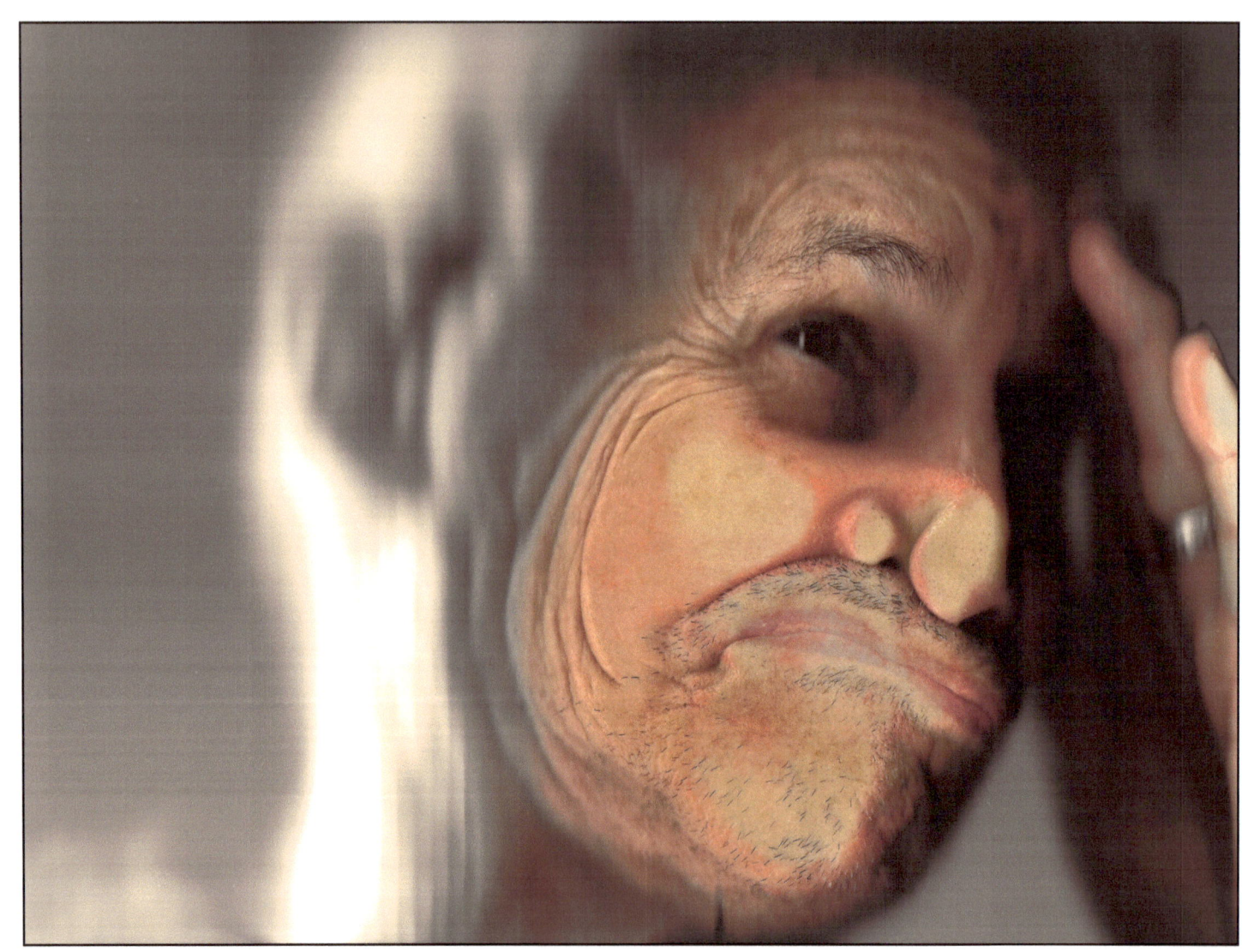

Day Fifteen: I'm Melting

At 6:30 a.m. the phone rings. They left a message. Back to sleep but not without bother. Who's on the phone? What are they doing calling me at 6:30? I am speculating and in and out of sleep. Must get up and see.

Finally, at 10 a.m., I give up. The cab company called, wanted me to come in, lots of folks waiting for rides, they need me. No, they need to keep their contract with the medical providers and others to provide timely service. More drivers on the road, good for the company, better pickup times, etc.

"Haven't seen you since the 18th" the voice said. "Come on in, lots of fares waiting."

But these days I'm the wind and I say when the wind blows. These fellas can dance all they want, but I'm leading the dance. I call out the moves, like the old guy on stage at a square dance.

That's right, cause on the 18th I made $35, which comes out to $4 an hour and some change for eight hours. Not really angry about it, though. It's just the way it is in the taxi world. But I want to create a better world for me. So it seems appropriate to put my photo series, "Miracles and Transformation," out there.

Thanks to the work I have doing, here in my crazy melting mind, I can move forward without to much resistance from the insiders, those pesky mind-fellas who ride in my head like leaves on the wind. Swirling, spinning and turning randomly at will.

But these days I'm the wind and I say when the wind blows. These fellas can dance all they want, but I'm leading the dance. I call out the moves, like the old guy on stage at a square dance.

Grab your partner, dosey doe.

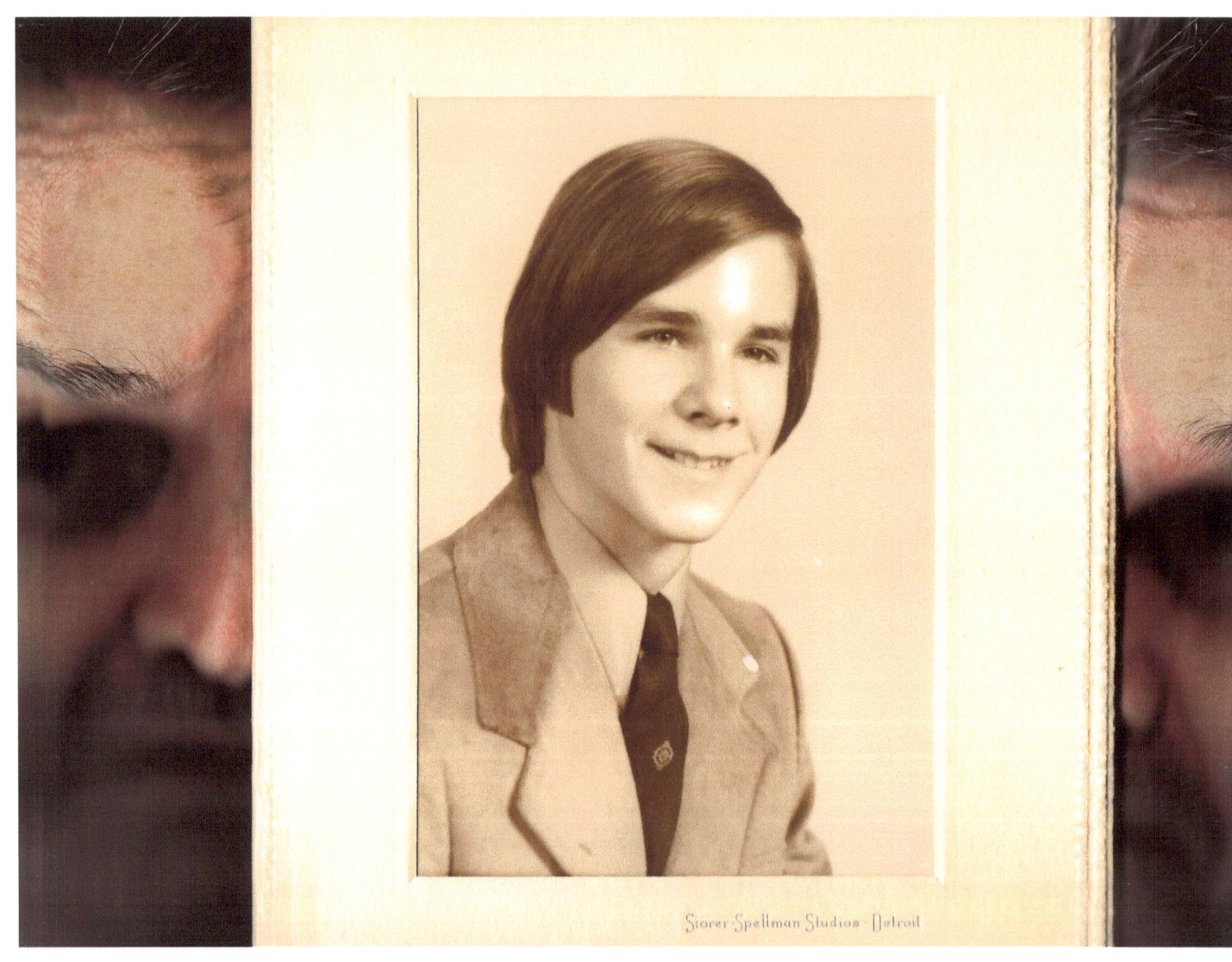

Storer-Spellman Studios - Detroit

Day Sixteen: Time Traveler

Yep, that's me on the left from 1972.

Spent the morning and part of the night time traveling, looking for answers. Asked a few questions, got a few answers.

Sometimes the answer comes down to a single event. Then one can build on that event and get more information. The things nightmares are made of.

Like the time he pulled me into the bathroom so he could do what others made him do. If my anger could rush out of me it would blow a hole in the computer and explode the house into a trillion pieces.

It may still be to early to speak of such things, such horrors.

And it does explode out of me, not in the way I want. I mean as in me, the real person, who I am, have been and always will be. Want to be, working to be. Events get in the way.

It may still be to early to speak of such things, such horrors. To release the monster, to let go of the control, to allow the killing spree. Feels good to recognize and realize the "me," the "I in Me." The "real me" knows these words can be said without harm without intent.

They are spoken as a way to escape the monster, the horrors, one of the many events that flavor my life. Digging them up, rediscovering, feeling, hating, pissing life away for lack of understanding or love or help or doorways to hell.

And do the words need to be revealed? Maybe, maybe not. It seems like they were once. The little boy went downstairs and told his parents and the parents of the other, of the monster, of the misguided sick, tormented being .

The event that plays out in the night as sleep sets in, as the dreams pull and push and terrify and spin and just fuck you up. The lifelong event that gets revisited consciously and unconsciously. That night time movie that gets replayed in silence over, and over, and fucking over again.

That fucking movie has a flavor, I can taste it. The horrible haunting sensation that has no place to go, nowhere to escape to, except in rage. The raging poison, the deadly venom. The infection that manifests itself into the art of living.

Maybe it's time to say the words.

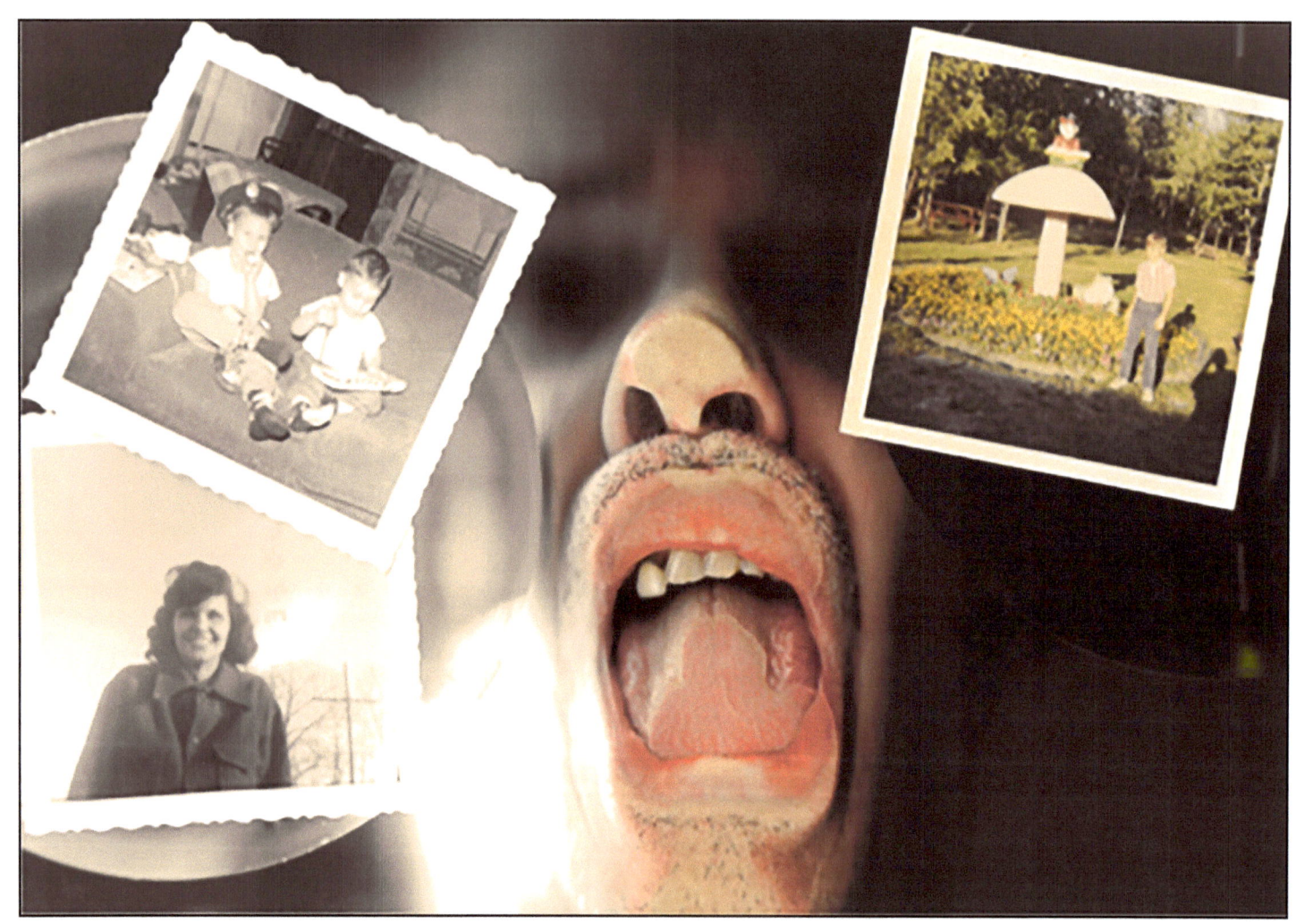

Day Seventeen: Mother's Day, Again

Mother's Days come and go without notice except for the commercial connections and social media mania. If your mother is dead she is still supposed to be mentioned or honored, even if she was a bad Mom in some way.

Isn't this the dilemma? How can anyone say they hate their mom? It's not easy but I said it a few times. Not out loud, just sort of quietly, without notice. I'm the only one who knows. That's okay that it was said, cause my mom taught me how to speak those words. She taught me how to hate, and be rotten and be bad and be everything I had to be to survive, which is all of the above.

She pissed me off, literally. Like the phrase, "Piss off." Go away, get out of here, disappear. This is where I really learned the phrase "Fine. Fuck you." Every time I say that, I'm talking to my mother.

She died in 1979. I had a love/hate relationship with her. But she's gone so it's over. I'm relieved. I don't have to fake it or pretend to love her. She actually really messed me up. Not on purpose though. It took me years to learn this and ultimately I forgave her for being a bad Mom.

I don't fucking know. I just pretend what I say matters and hope for the best. Sometimes it feels real, other times I don't trust a word I'm hearing or saying.

The conflict, however, still lingers and it's with me on a daily basis in various ways. Not the idea of her being a bad Mom, but the fact that her actions attributed to my own bad behavior.

It's a ball rolling down an endless hill. Really no way to stop it, just have to learn how to watch it roll by and stay out of the way. But isn't that the trick to living or staying alive? Learning how to stay out of the way of yourself.

I don't fucking know. I just pretend what I say matters and hope for the best. Sometimes it feels real, other times I don't trust a word I'm hearing or saying. Perhaps this is why these days I have difficulty speaking coherently. Quite often I stumble through sentences trying to say what I think I mean.

Maybe I don't really know anything?

Well, that's stupid. Everyone knows something. See, it's this back and forth, and back and forth, and back and forth, and back and forth.

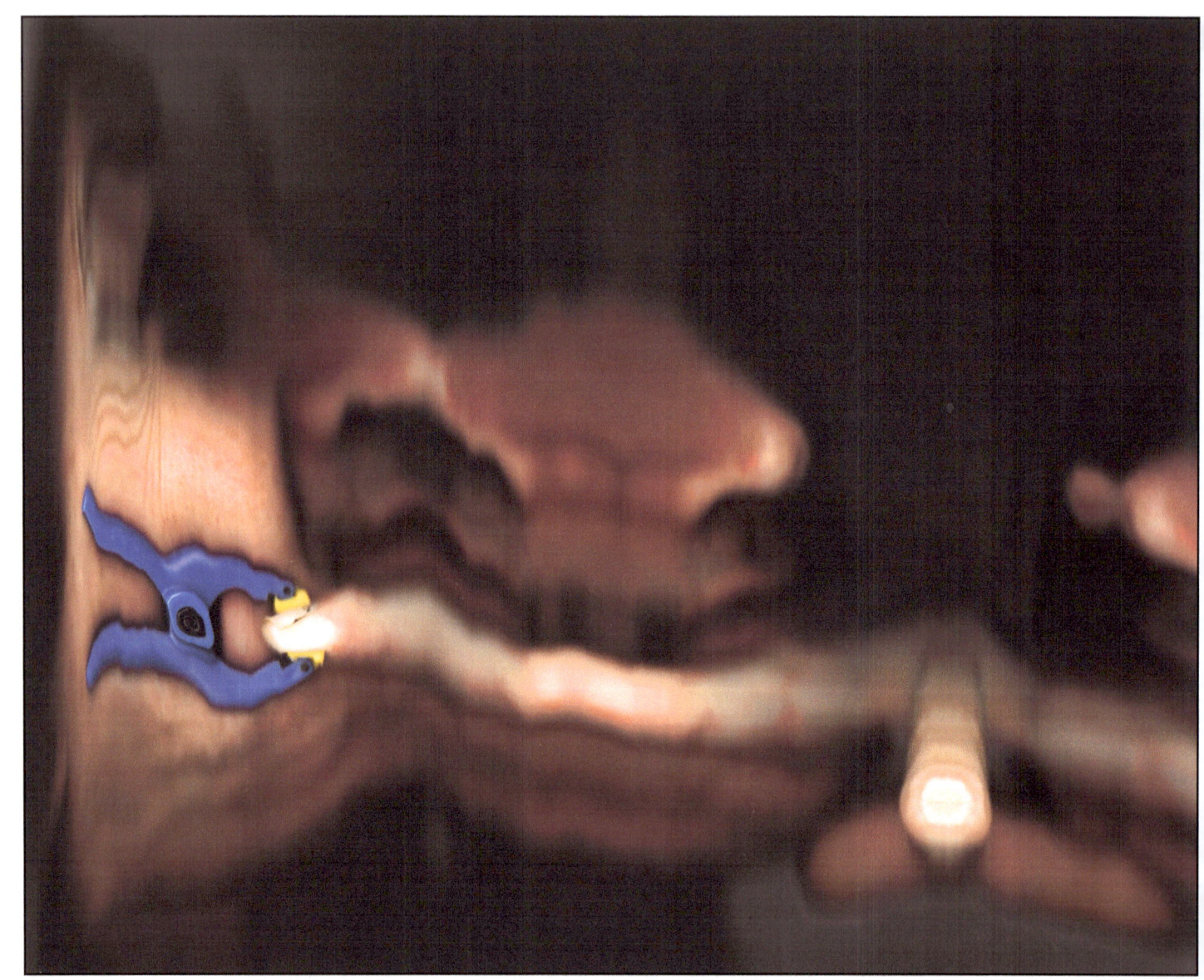

Day Eighteen: Hell and Back

Up one day, down the next. How far down is the question. To Hell seems appropriate. Feels like too much in the way to even consider sorting it all out. As each word rolls out in front of me I seem to be getting closer to a temporary resolve, or not.

One more cup of coffee, one more day, one more hour, one more of everything before the crap hits the fan.

Last night I thought about shooting my toe off. That's a new one. Maybe it's comic relief after all the mind bending work taking place.

Strange days indeed.

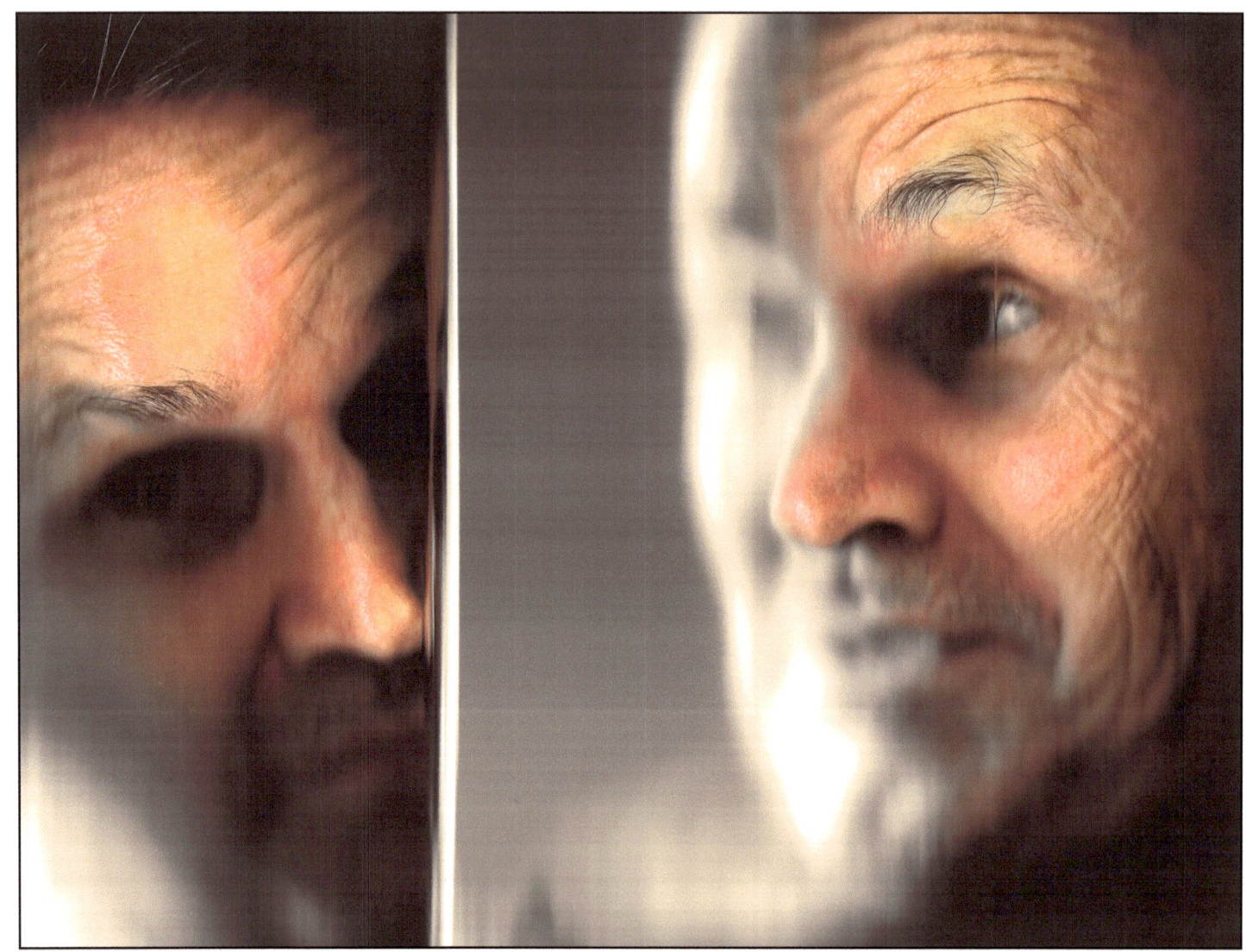

Day Nineteen: Two-Faced Motherfucker

If an image could describe depression, this may be it. In the back of the head, behind the eyes lay the demons from hell. Up front, the face struggles to be presentable.

The conflict this creates hurts.

The idea of going out there and facing people is horrific. Just leave me be. Let me be here in this space free from any obligation to be correct or socially acceptable or bathed or clean-shaved. Just let me be. Let the demons work their way through my head until they have had enough play time and get exhausted.

The demons can have their say and they can play and play, but I'm still in control. If I want to shut them up I go to sleep. Staying awake and active is the ultimate challenge.

What the fuck else can be done? Just sit and wait and try to be nice or stay in control. Actually staying in control is easy as long as there are no obligations to be in a particular space or time. To be other than the demons.

The demons can have their say and they can play and play, but I'm still in control. If I want to shut them up I go to sleep. Staying awake and active is the ultimate challenge.

Eat little pieces of reality. Tiny pieces. Enough to sustain life. Just stay alive for one more day.

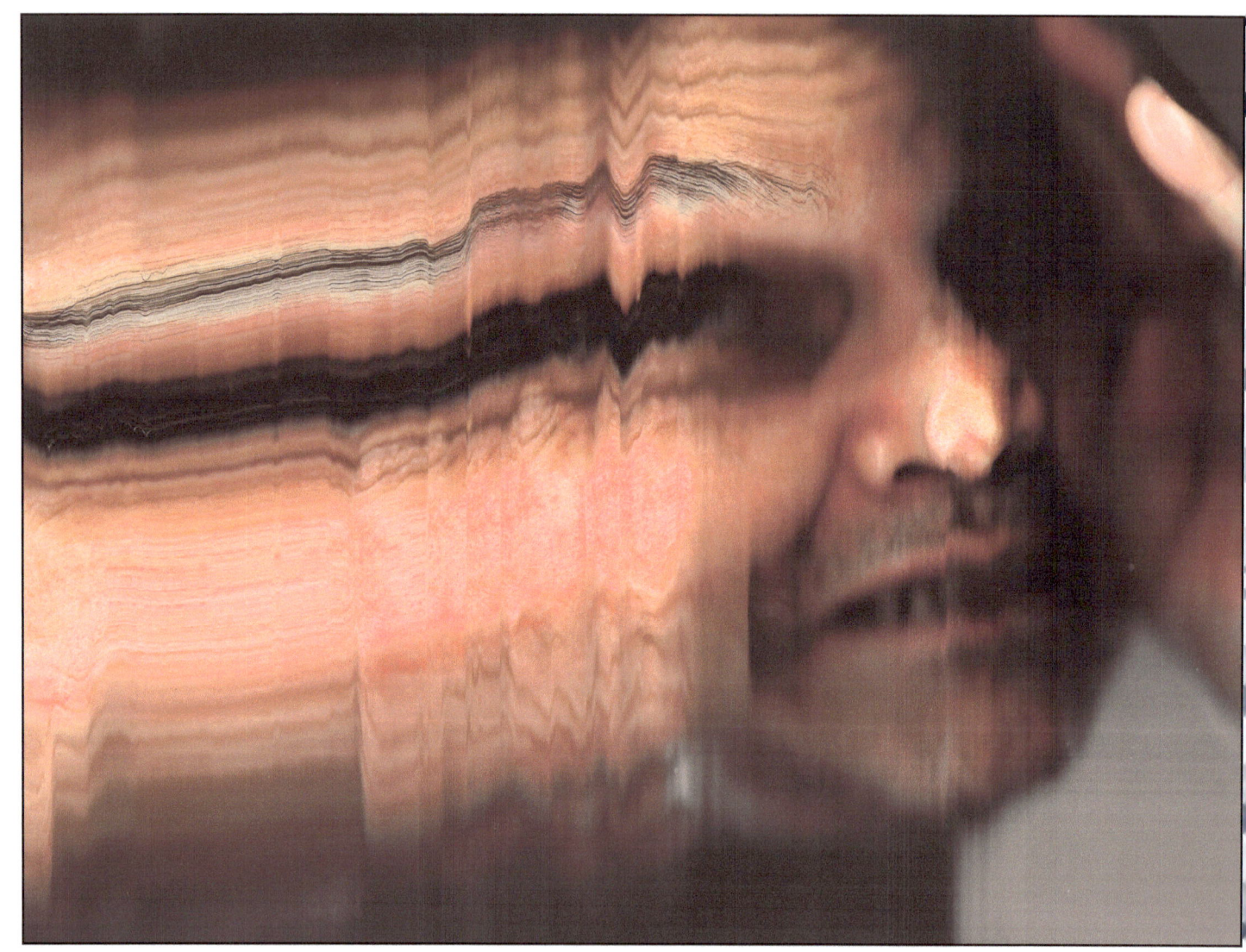

Day Twenty: Mr. Stretchy, You're fucked!

I don't have a gun cause I would use it, maybe, to shoot myself. If I did not say maybe and instead said, "I would shoot myself," then that is what would happen. So leaving "maybe" in there means there is still hope.

Hope for another day or minute or half hour. Hope for reprieve from the nagging emotional pain. There is no aspirin or medication to stop it. Hence the desire to use the gun. One shot, pain gone.

Dark-ass morbid revelations. Sickening. Who wants a dark-ass morbid sick individual to play with? "Okay, let's play, guys. Who can figure the best, quickest and less messy way to kill yourself?"

Feeling better, feeling worse. Up and down, up and down. There is no way out. Have to learn to walk the edges, silently so as not to wake the monsters. Walk gently with purpose and intention, be clear, be concise, be right on. Let everyone have their way. Don't resist.

Lick it up boy, eat the dust, breath it in. All those memories smashed into the dirt. The sub-atomic dust of living.

Buy a tree, build a tree-house. But really, just get out somehow. Not the way of the gun.

Scratch the paint from the wall. Look behind there. Pull the carpet from the floor, look under there. Lay in the 30 years of dirt stuck under there. Roll around, pretend it feels good. Foul yourself again.

Lick it up boy, eat the dust, breath it in. All those memories smashed into the dirt. The subatomic dust of living. Not a single memory to cherish, not a single one. Too fucking cold in the winter, too fucking hot in the summer, cracker-jack-box house all beat up and broken.

Home is an atomic bomb.

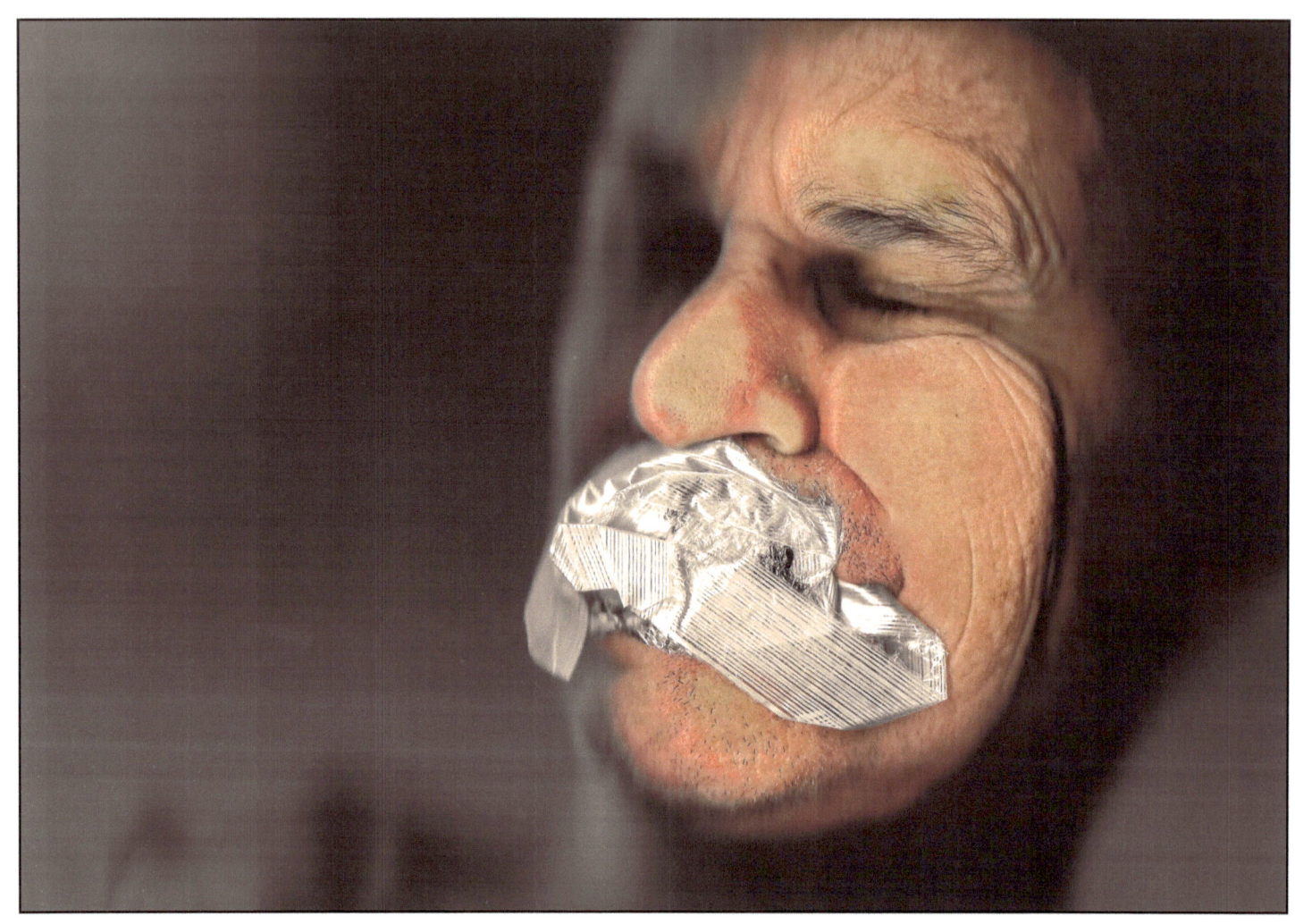

Day Twenty One: The Long Road Home

When one leaves home there is no going back. It's never the same. All was lost, misplaced, misrepresented. It's a foolish endeavor.

Out of bed, one foot in front of the other. Get up, boy. Get up. Turn the corner, look down the hall, walk to the living room. Look alright. Feel okay. Listen for the stirring, the motions of lost souls.

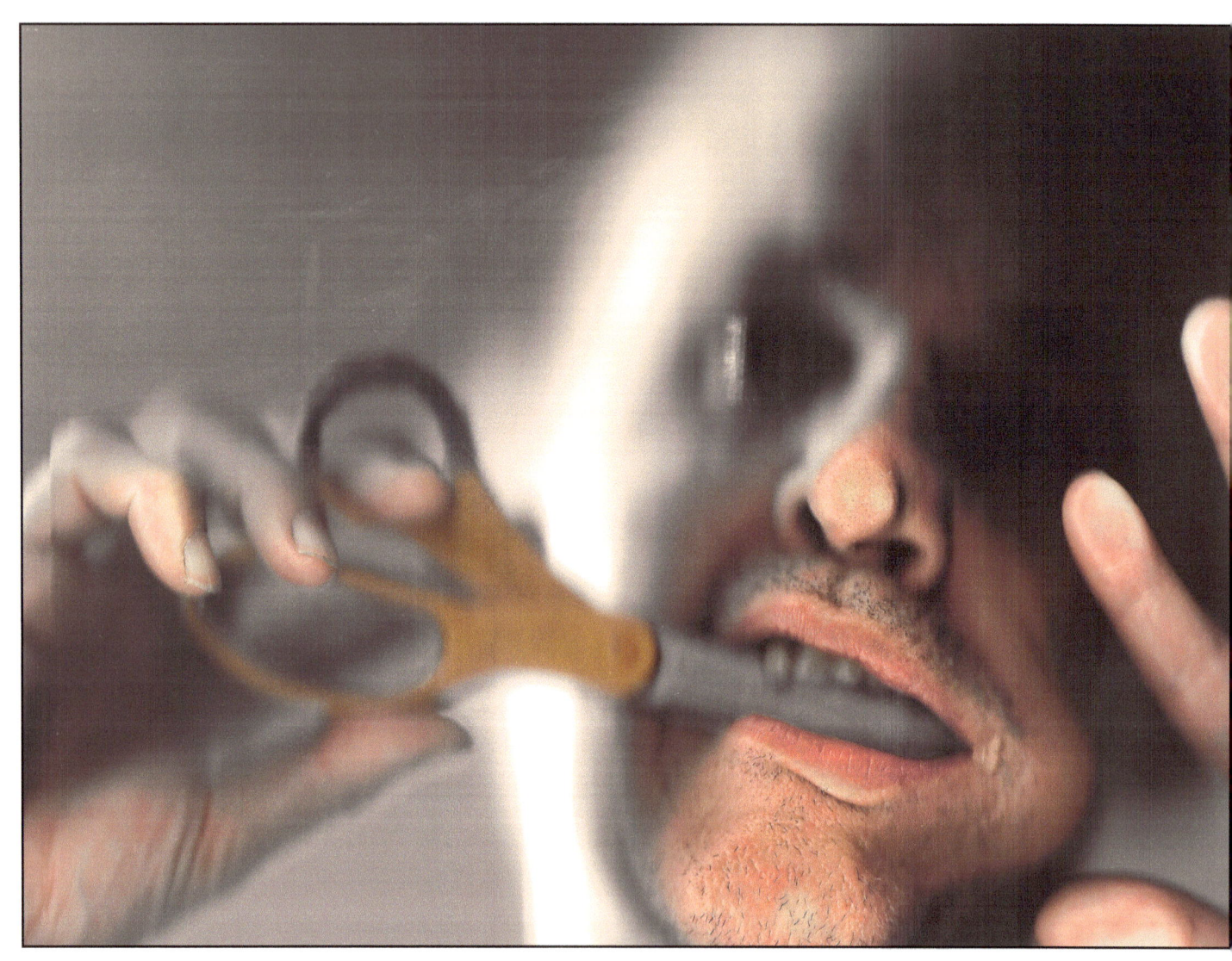

Day Twenty Two: The End?

Spitting out life and it comes back.

Unpleasant and furious.

It's in the middle, the center of the brain. That spot where the voice wants to get to. Stuck there, confidently. Every day, especially in the mornings, it calls out, like the Sirens who lured sailors to their death.

Only one way to get in. Have to tear it apart, rip it open, dig deep, stab, stab, cut, cut, piece by piece.

Once this week, maybe twice there was silence in my head. I had to remind myself the pain, the desire to go away, the death wish still exists. Seems comical, to remind oneself it's always time to die. As if death is the door for rescue and is always unlocked.

It takes awhile to get out of bed. To reconcile with the Lord of Death. "Not now, never." It's a nuisance, a morning ritual. Feels like a right of passage, like a way to move closer to life instead of embracing death.

Every day, each morning it's always there, waiting. The end. Looking at the words here I realize my life has value and it will never end foolishly. That monster in my head will live on cause the imprint is stronger than life. The idea that there is a resolve is silly and naive.

It's a learning process, it is not the end.

Let it live and let it play. Cause when it dies, I'm dead. Things happen in life that can never be erased. I'm branded, my brain is branded. A memory so deep and vibrant it will always prevail. Imagine an incident so potent that it can alter the brain chemistry.

Imagine reliving the horror every day. Feeling it, knowing how fucked up and horrible it was and no one was there to stop it. Even though they were in another part of the house. Even though they were told and chose to ignore. Not a word, not a peep, not a single acknowledgment.

It must have been an invisible happening. It did not exist. Yes it did, I was there. I'm still here.

It's a learning process, it is not the end.

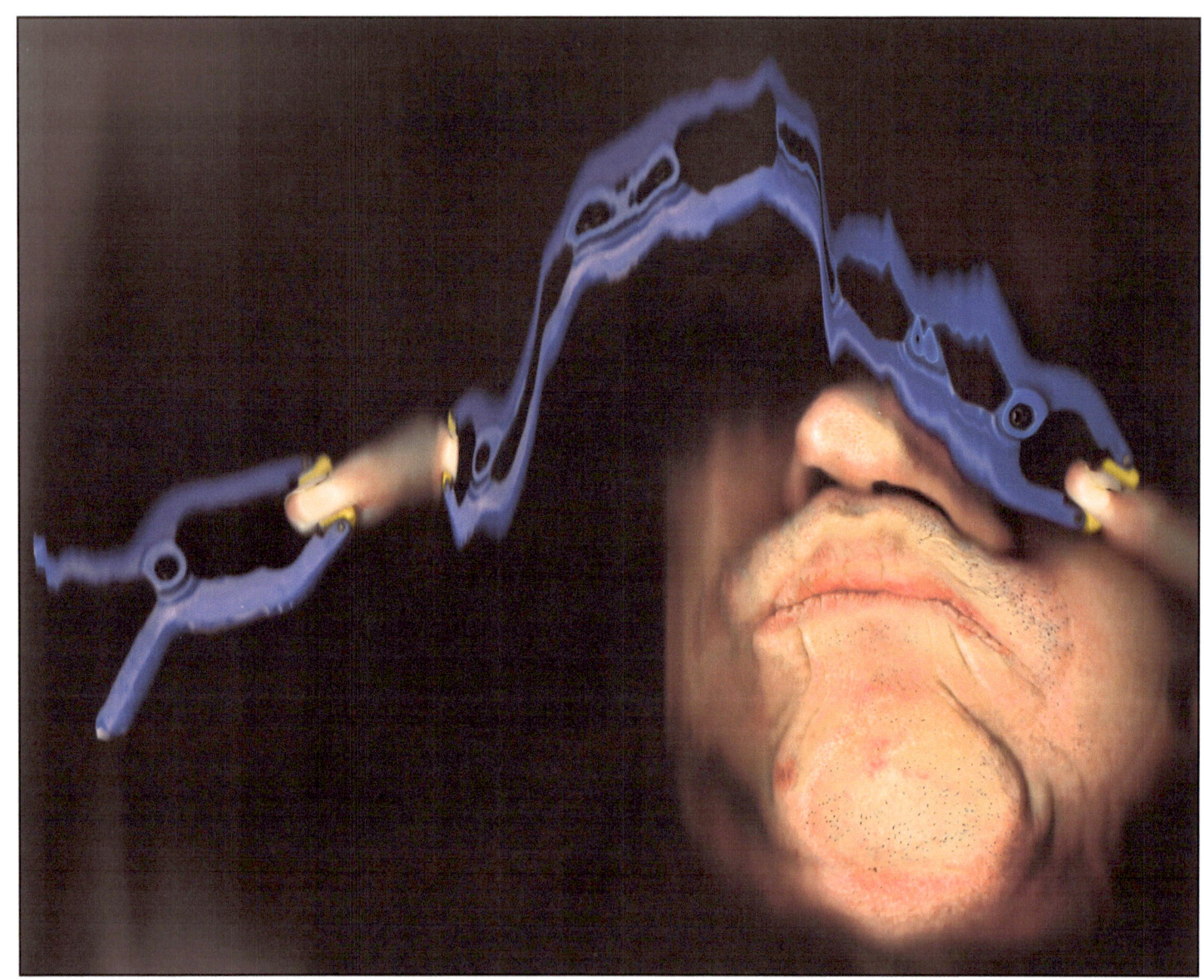

Day Twenty Three: Just A Little Horrible

Bed feels so good, sleep feels so good, yummy, yummy.

The idea of digging for the problem, tearing it out with sharp edges dominates.

The horror of getting out of bed, knowing or not knowing whether Mr. Depression will follow my footsteps from the bed to the bathroom and everywhere I walk.

Knowing that thing is living in my head is crazy. Like naming a cake "New and Improved Insane Cake." Just for you, today only. $9.99. Every day, every day, every day.

I'm free and feeling good, hope prevails.

It's 12:47p.m. The crazy in my head is humming quietly, just making enough noise to remind me of its presence.

So at this time of day the crazy and I make a deal. You let me do my thing and I'll let you exist. So now for the rest of the day I have to be aware that the crazy is there, but I'm free from it because of our deal.

I'm free and feeling good, hope prevails.

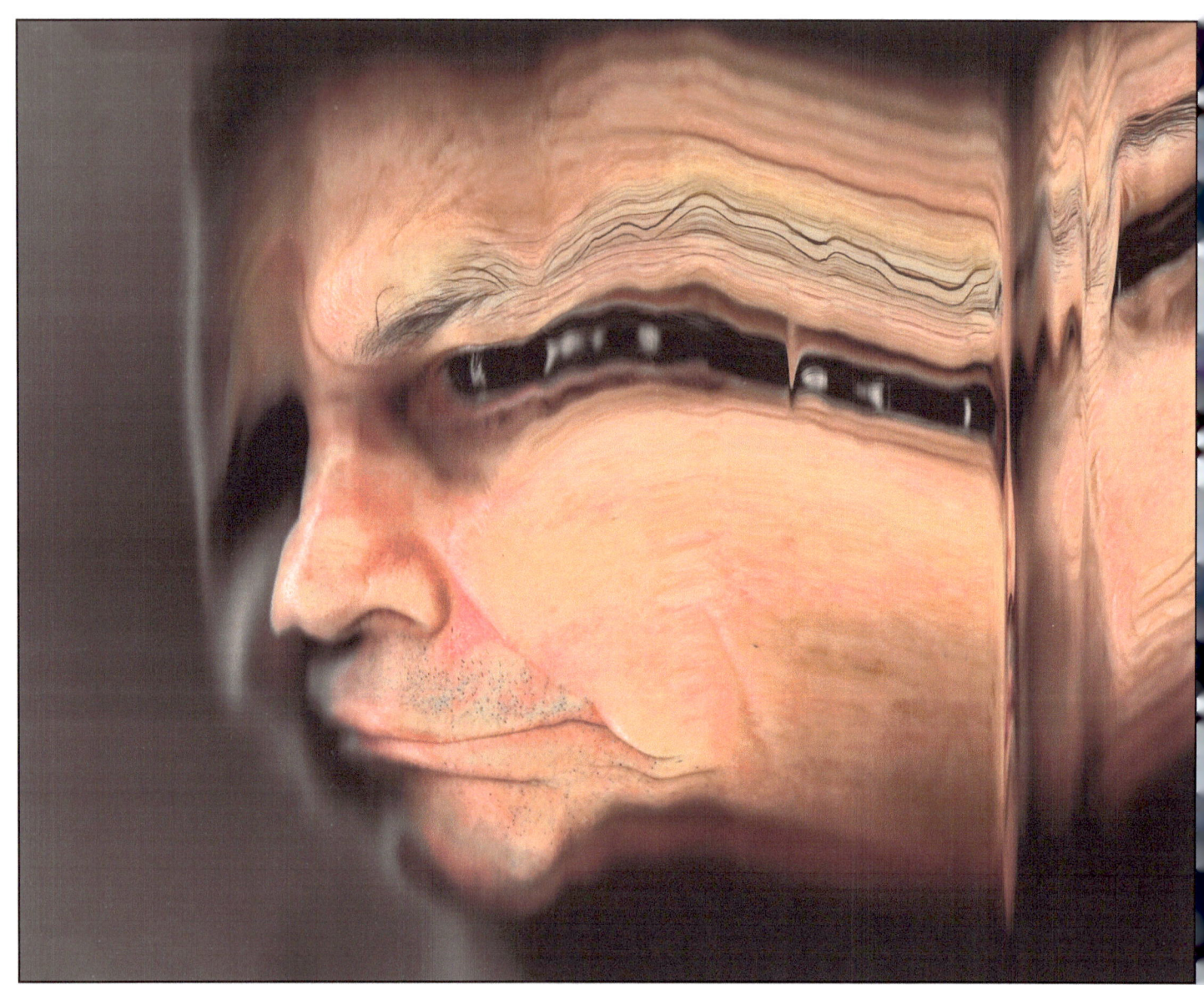

Day Twenty Four: Puzzle Master

Every day is another day. A place to begin again. From morning until night the puzzle has to be worked on. It feels like a sacred endeavor, a quest for peace, love and joy. Just as the divine wanted. An everlasting quest for ourselves.

How do we survive, how are we going to die, then what? Working to play, living to die.

Each piece of the puzzle represents the way forward. Slapping the pieces down, moving them all around is progress.

If we put up enough sticky notes things will change. You are not human unless you suffer. We become pleasant after we suffer, even thankful.

I must have suffered enough this week. Pleasantness is knocking at my door.

Each piece of the puzzle represents the way forward. Slapping the pieces down, moving them all around is progress. Every day another piece should fall into place. The more the pieces fit the less one suffers.

It's a puzzle with a million pieces. Always start at the beginning, one foot in front of the other.

Walk on, crazy boy, walk on.

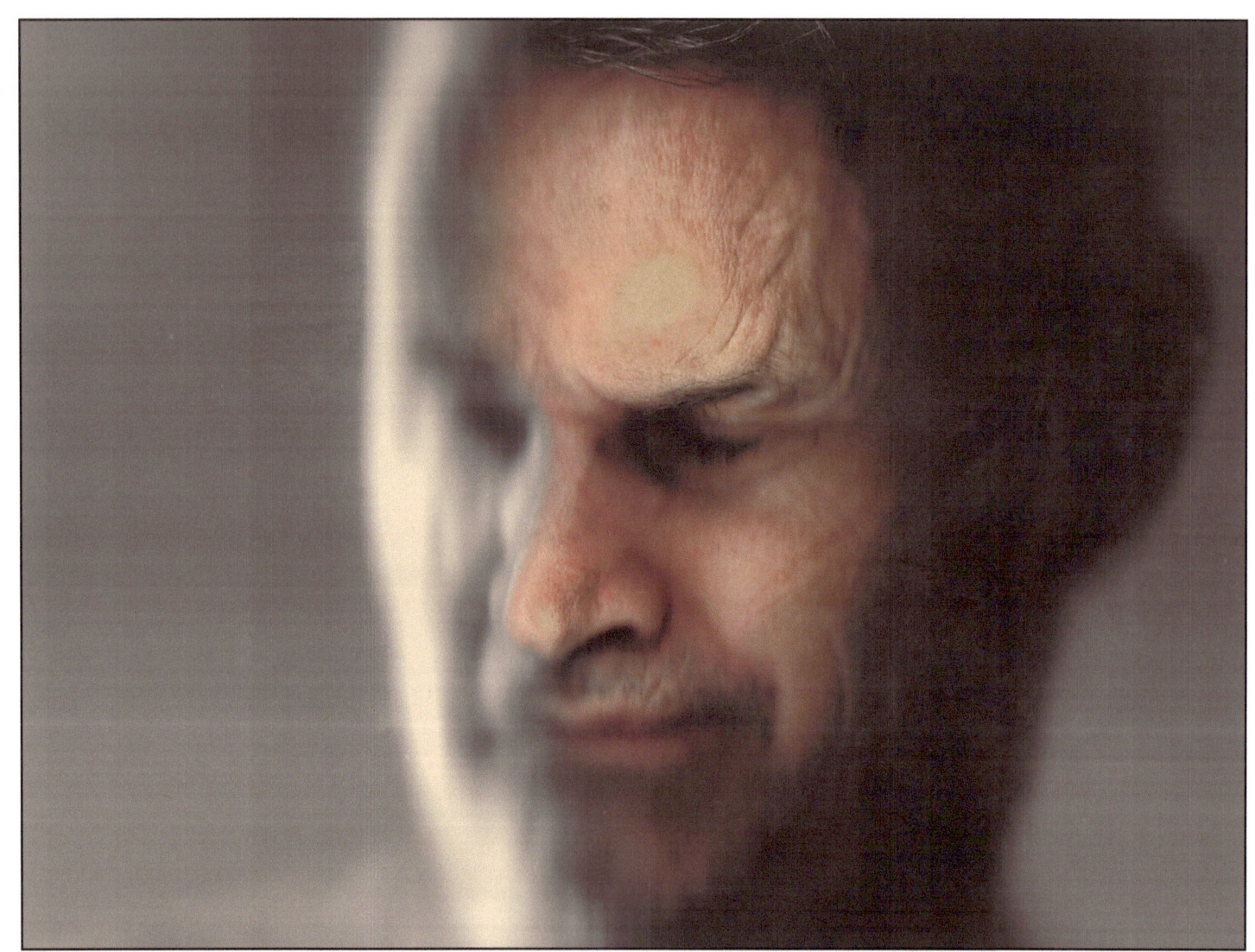

Day Twenty Five: Therapeutic Endeavor

Becoming more challenging to come here and look then examine myself. Perhaps it's the neutral ground, that place that says everything is alright you can stop now. Or maybe it's the same old program, the trickster Coyote.

All I know right now is I'm very tired, need to sleep. Good night.

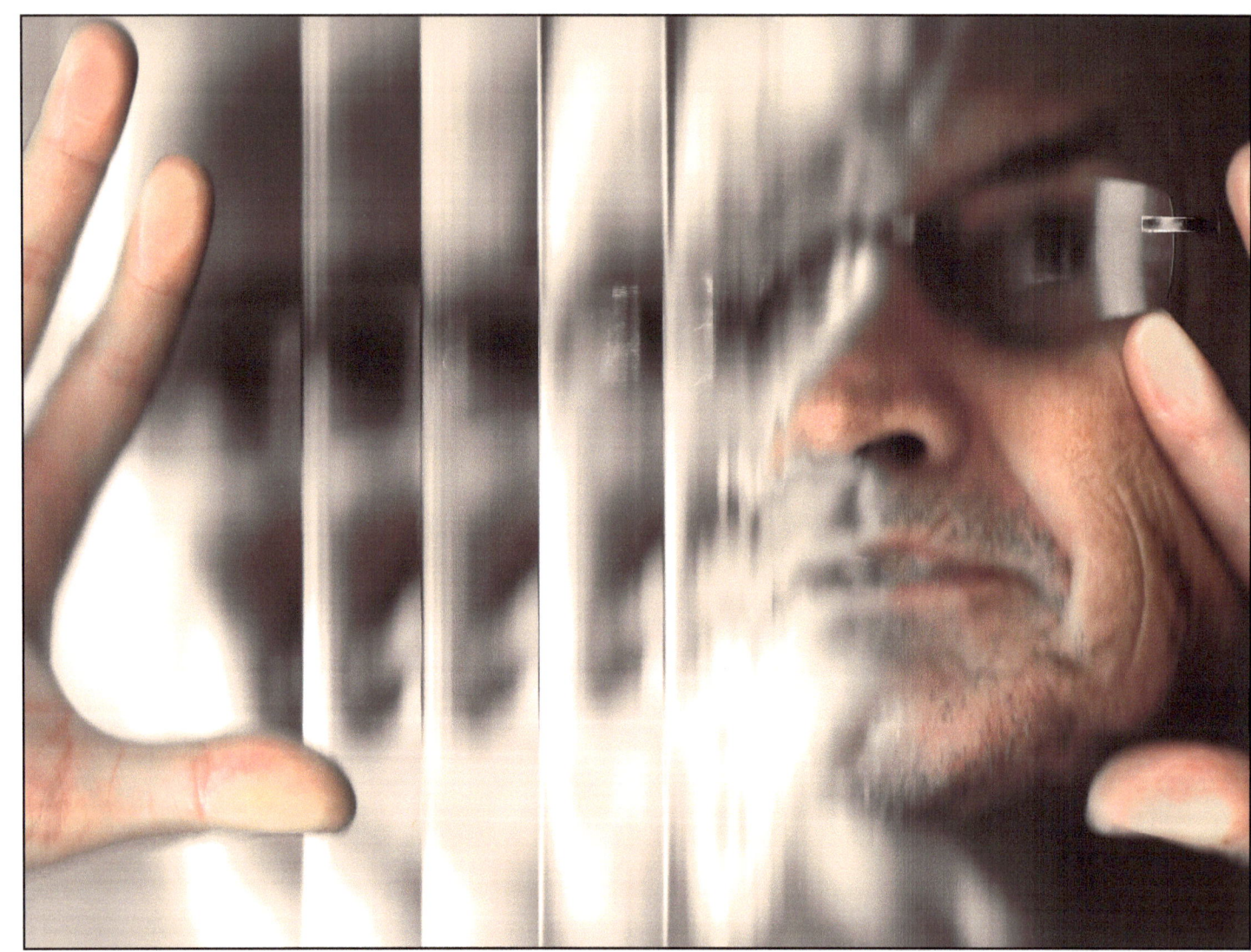

Day Twenty Six: Who Am I?

Feels like two of me, sometimes three, roaming around in my head.

"Clowns to the left of me, jokers to the right. Here I am, stuck in the middle with you."

Beatles, sometime in my life.

Every word, thought and action must be checked. Slows things down. It's a nice slow. Feels good, especially when the desired words and actions occur.

Step 1. Receive incoming information.

Step 2. Control the output.

Step 3. Chose an appropriate response.

Have to move slow or else the other, the one I don't want to be, creeps in.

"I like myself and the Universe, we get along just fine. I been free since I hit the road, and I'll be free when I die. Swim the ocean, walk the coast, jump from rock to rock. I'll be free when I hit the road and I'll be free when I die."

Wrote this more than 30 years ago after leaving, running away, from home. The only way to escape is to run away. Then start looking for places to hide.

These days there are three of me. Each one has his own rules and regards the other with some sense of respect.

Hiding inside myself, sharing space with the craziness inside the mind. And it's like a thousand years have passed in a single second. A flash of the past so real but too quick to feel scared.

These days there are three of me. Each one has his own rules and regards the other with some sense of respect. The person I want to be, the person I am, has emerged and is in control. The others seem fine with this and don't put up much of a fight. We all get along, most of the time.

Must keep training each other for the big fight, cause we all know it's coming and we all know it is like a hurricane, twist you while you roll and shake you to the bone.

Or maybe the big one doesn't exist and only happens when I let it in. Something to continue to think about.

And the stabbing knives still exist.

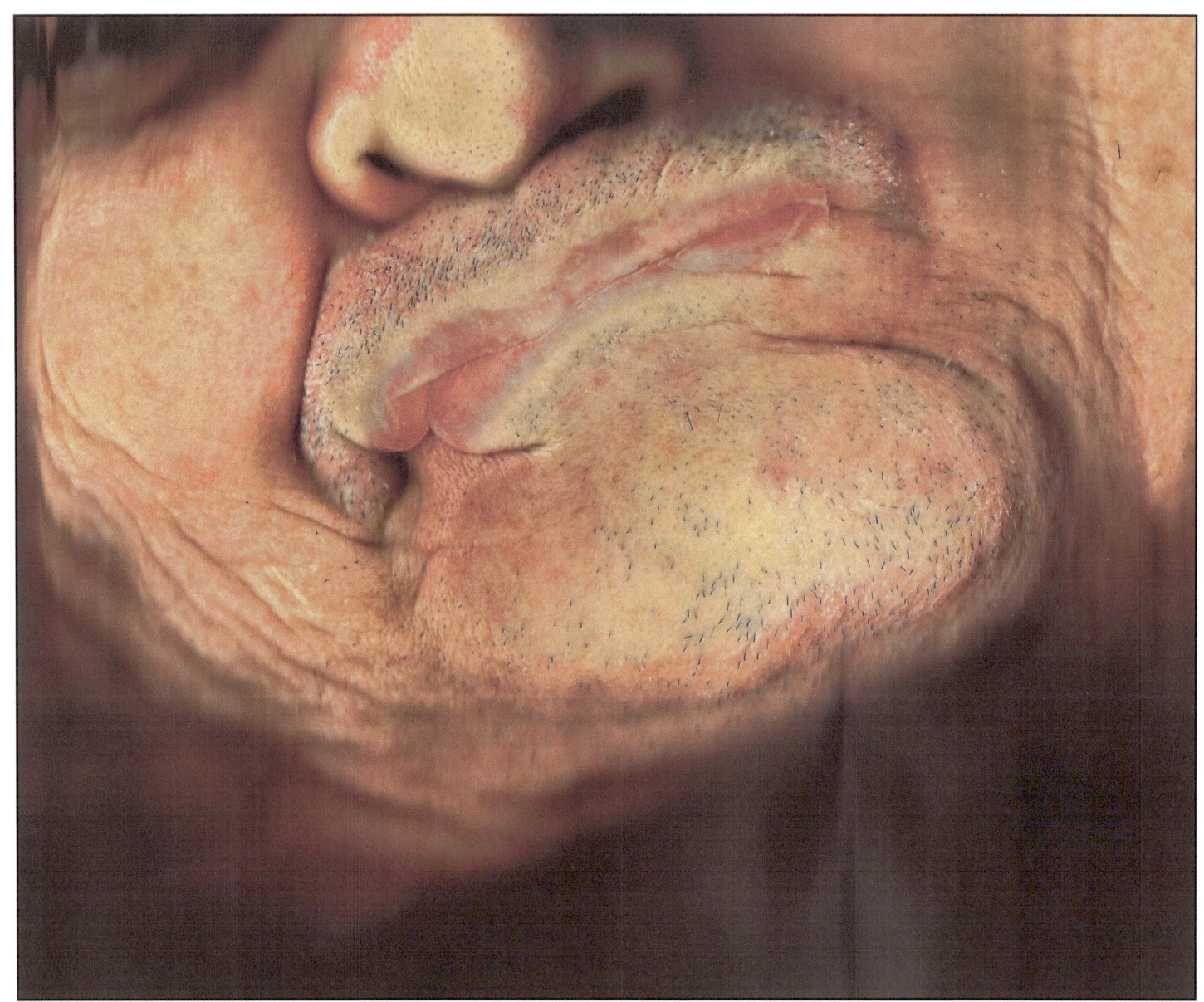

Day Twenty Seven: Dead Meat

"Go get some lunch. Come back after that, we should be done," said the doctor so casually as if the body on the table all cut up meant nothing. I ate lunch and came back. The doctor was done. "Don't need to photograph the brain, no significant damage."

That's good. Didn't want to see it anyway. His heart laying on the floor with surgical rods stuck through the shattered parts was enough.

The first time I photographed a dead body it was of a man who had drowned. The officer who requested the work sensed my hesitation. 'First One?" he said. "Yes" I answered.

He told me to touch the body. I did. He asked what it felt like. "Like a piece of cold meat," I replied.

"Good. Treat all the bodies like dead cold meat and you'll be fine," he said without hesitation.

The body had eyes and they were open. The dead man was screaming for help, his eyes told the story of death, how it feels to know you are going to die, the horror and pain all mixed together.

I came to terms with being a photographer of the dead. Living felt different after that. Living and being alive seemed like a special experience, one that should be guarded, cherished and appreciated.

Part of my job in the Marine Corps was to photograph dead bodies for police investigations. I saved all the pictures and took them home on leave, like trophies. Just a few people saw them. Enough to make me realize I had been twisted by the experiences. I burned them in the back yard. I came to terms with being a photographer of the dead. Living felt different after that. Living and being alive seemed like a special experience, one that should be guarded, cherished and appreciated.

Perhaps this is why I could never pull the trigger and take my own life. It's good to be alive.

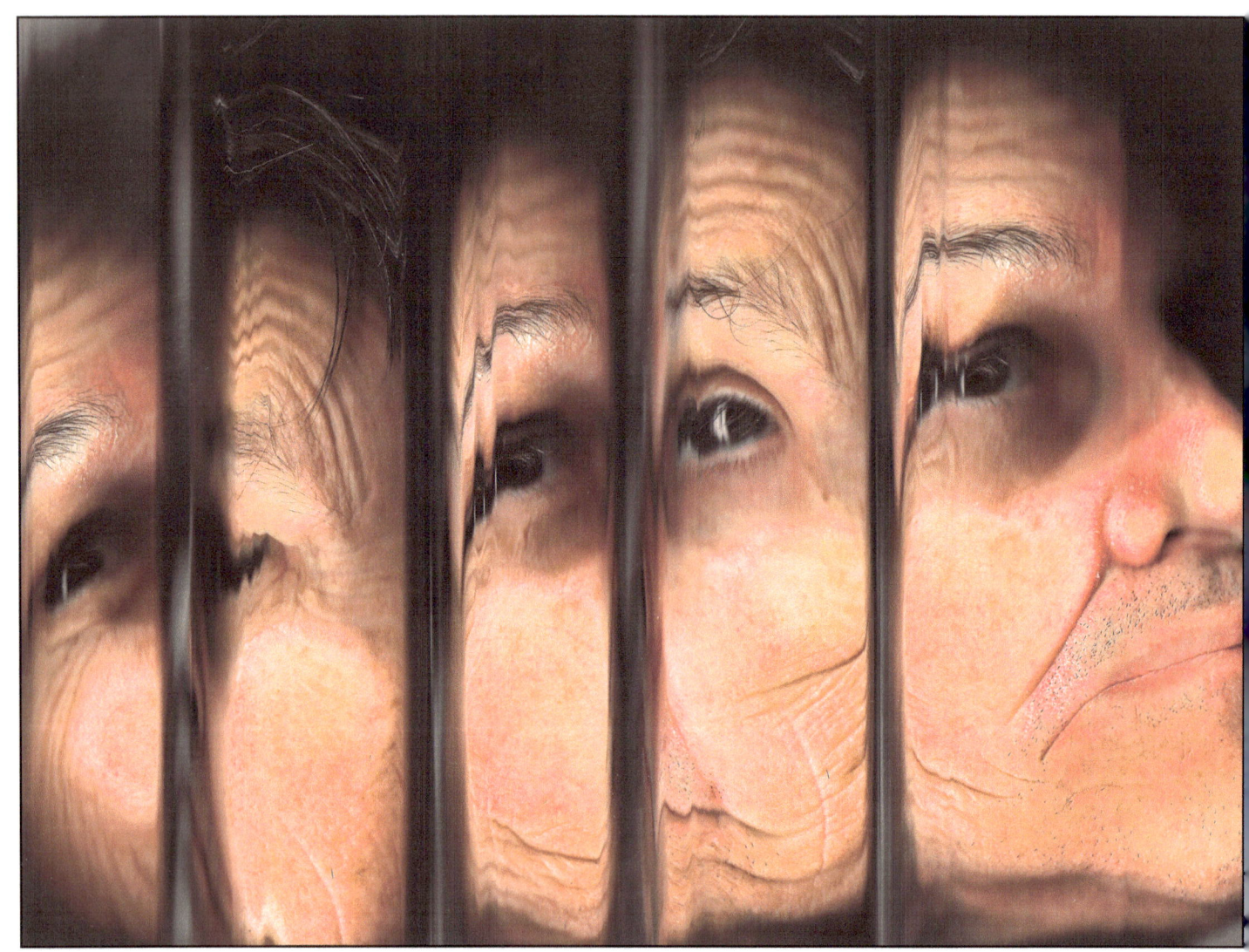

Day Twenty Eight: Conflicted

"Standing at the door between leaving and gone," From a song by Pj. McArdle circa1980.

What is happening in my life now has happened many times before. This time, however, I chose to react appropriately. It's not a quick reaction. It has to be steady and measured, as in how we live, how our bodies breathe, and how we manage the complexities of being human. Although steady and measured is an ideal way to manage ourselves, for me it has felt impossible.

Sometimes I feel like a wrecking ball in motion. It cannot be stopped and has to demolish all that gets in its way. This wrecking-ball approach to life no longer dominates my being. I am the one in control and I decide which pedal to push or lever to pull to move the ball forward. And it has taken most of my adult life to get here. Not an easy road but it's good to be home.

Still, there are conflicts. And every day almost every hour decisions have to be made on how to react appropriately. This gets complicated cause our behavior is learned and we are taught what is appropriate. Although I have always known right from wrong and what is good or bad. Knowing and doing are not the same, however.

So now I have to revisit the place that less than three months ago caused me to go crazy. Or as my wife says, "A psychotic break from reality."

It was not the first time I had lost my mind. But it was for me the scariest. Hence my desire to fix things was reawakened. I have been in and out of therapeutic programs and on and off antidepressants most of my adult life. This time, however, was the final call, my last chance to fix myself, to reprogram my brain. Why? Because I wanted to learn what love is and how to live with love in my life, not anger, discontent, worry, fear and all the other negative energies I felt comfortable with. The crazy in me has to go.

So here I am again, "Standing at the door between leaving and gone." Every little thing that months ago would flip me out has been knocking at the door. I have been able to answer the door and invite the monsters in, and even have coffee and donuts with them.

I had been prepping for this for years as I jumped from therapy to medication and off medication and back to therapy. Each time I began to feel better I would fool myself and stop the medication and therapy.

Isn't it odd that the only time one has problems is when someone else says that they have a problem.

But anyway, all these experiences taught me how to approach the issues and seek professional help. I have accepted the fact that I will have to be vigilant and stay in tune with myself. Keep myself clear, unobstructed, and free from the influences of my old programming.

How I live in a crazy world is up to me. It's good to know love intimately as opposed to hanging around with anger, hate and discontent.

The old program exists but the newer one is stable and will remain and continue to consume and take control over the old one. I say this with complete confidence. I say this because it is what I have learned.

"What I tell myself is what I will believe."

It's sounds like a simple solution and it is. To do the reprogramming, changing the belief system, controlling and choosing appropriate reactions. I wanted to shed the old me and bring out the real me, the one I truly enjoy being and the one others can stand being around.

How I live in a crazy world is up to me. It's good to know love intimately as opposed to hanging around with anger, hate and discontent. There are infinite pathways one could travel but only one path gets picked at any given time. I chose peace, love, joy and gratitude.

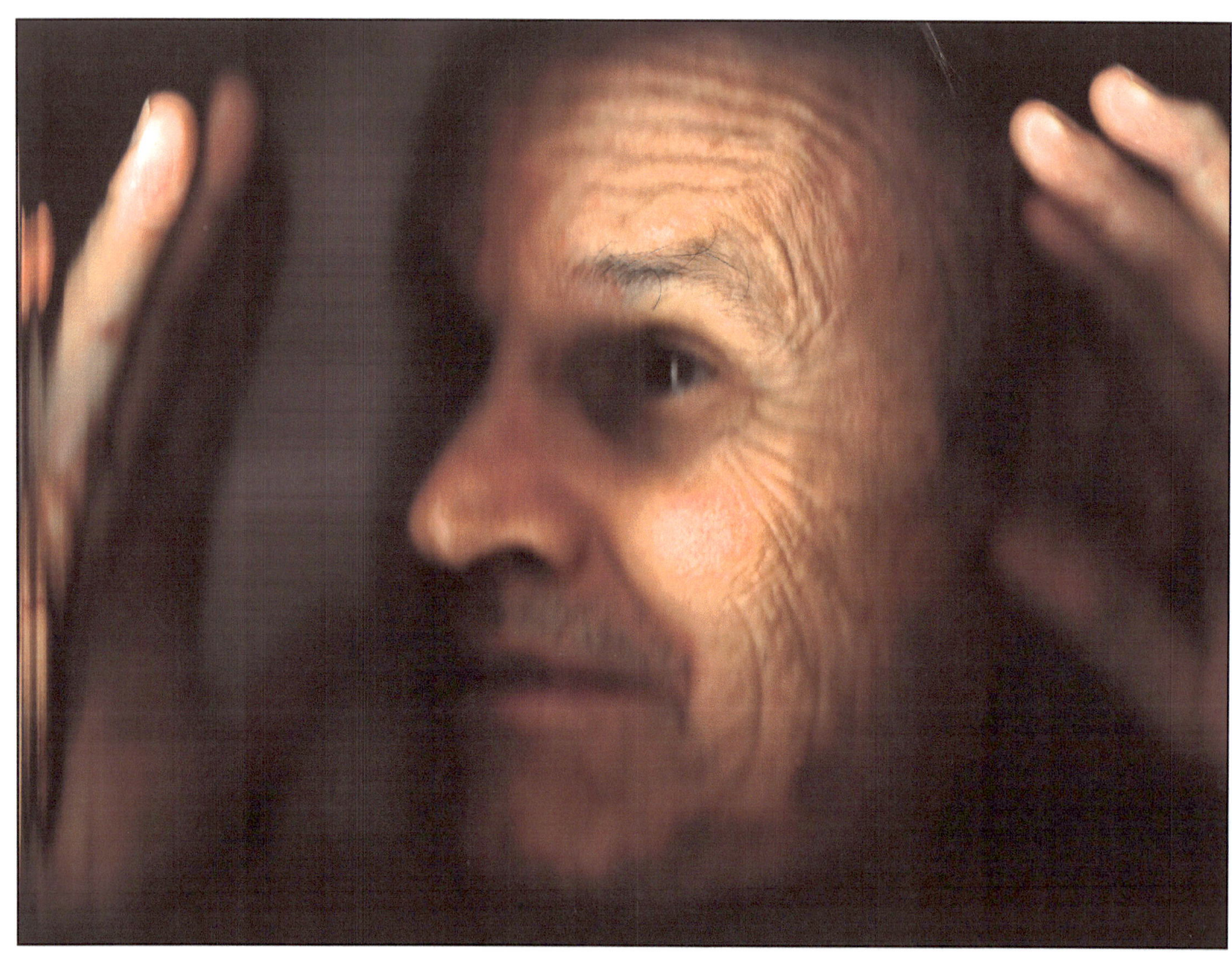

Day Twenty Nine. Close To Happy Face

It feels like I'm on the other side of darkness. The reprogramming is working. Must stay vigilant. Every day, every minute, always, all the time and for the rest of my life, must stay vigilant.

The old program, pjmac.5.0, has been upgraded to pjmac.10.0. Ten is the best. It's at the top. I deserve it.

Putting words in my head, only positive ones. Every word makes a difference. Spend a day saying peace, love, joy and gratitude, and see how it works. It's miraculous and rewarding.

Words in my head are sweet like flowers in my bed. (Silly me.)

So on this twenty ninth day I say congratulations to me.

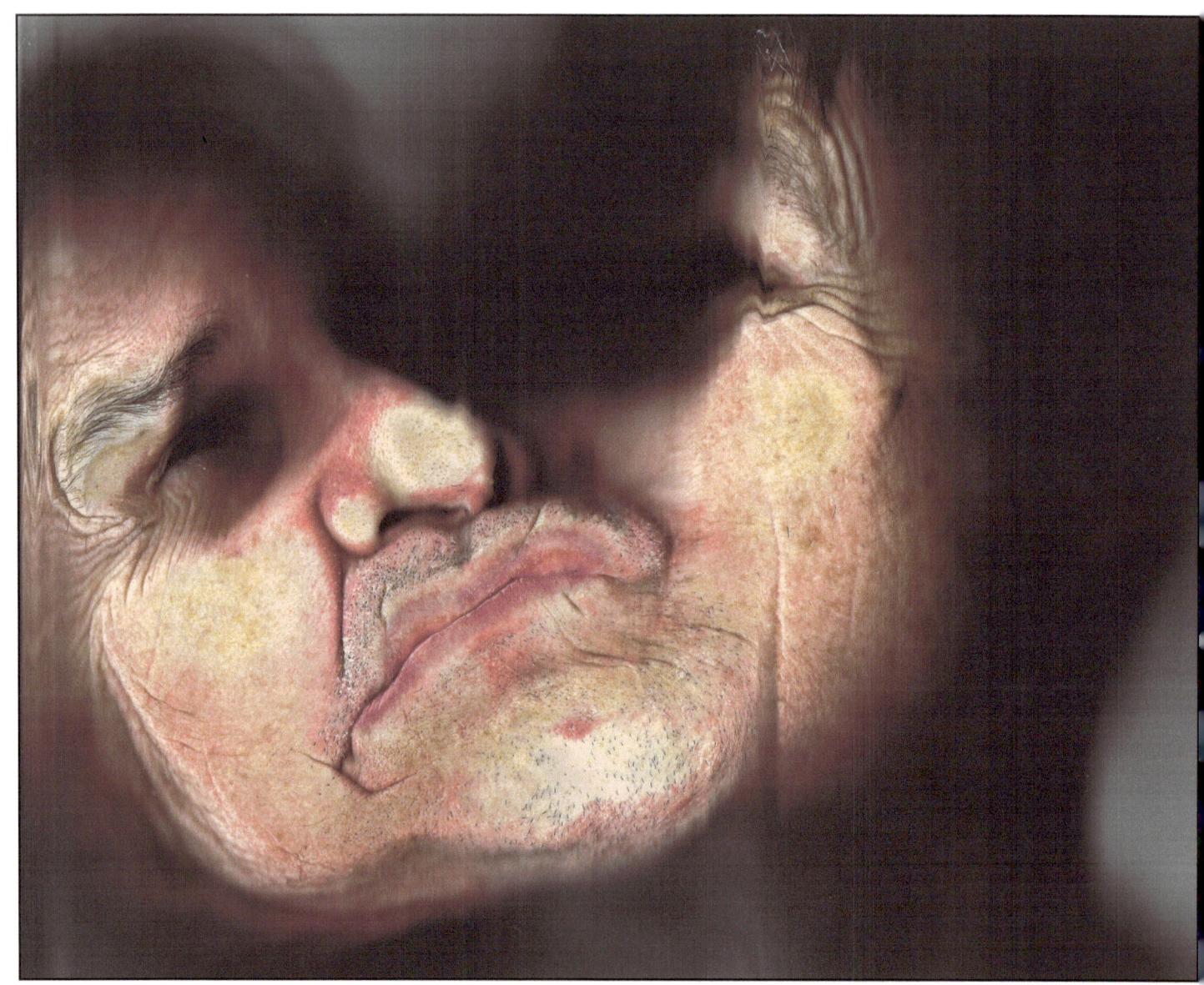

Depression Diaries: Again

According to the last page the depression is over. Bullshit. It will never be out of my life. I sit here staring at the image and ask why? It does not matter, get used to it, learn to live with it.

I am, one day at a time.

It has taken four weeks to come back to my Depression Diaries. I thought I was done exploring, which meant the depression was also gone. So my wife read the diaries and pointed a few things out. It was then I realized once again I fooled myself into believing I was good to go.

The exploration was done, all the depression would stay on those pages and go away.

Can't say yes, can't say no.

Axes grinding out back.

Chop, chop, another whack.

Looking at the image I realize there are two of me. The person I am and the person I can be.

I fooled myself into thinking I could chose which one walks in my shoes. That's so wrong, denial in its highest form.

So, hell no, my depression is not gone. And hopefully I will know better than to think or fool myself into believing it will never return. It is living and has intention.

It's like, "Look, I'm out of bed. I'm walking and responding and not killing myself." And so goes the day. Carefully maneuvering through the shit piles of life. (And I don't really mean "shit piles of life. I love living and life.) But that is how it can be. Constantly scrutinizing every thought, every word. Trying to reprogram and reset practically all of my being. Or rather trying to put the depression into a storage locker. A place that is safe for it and me.

Depression is like a person with its own agenda, its own ideas and beliefs. If it is not recognized the depression can erase who we really are. It can destroy us by not killing. It can eat into us and crawl under our skin and make us ache and cry and want to die. And depression always has its finger on the trigger. It is always there, a constant reminder that I am not alone.

So, hell no, my depression is not gone. And hopefully I will know better than to think or fool myself into believing it will never return. It is living and has intention. After all these years I have finally learned the best I can do is learn how to get along with the depression.

And get along does not mean be best friends. It simply means to control, recognize and react appropriately to its everlasting power. There are ways to reprogram and reset my brain so depression is not in control. I will continue to learn as time passes.

"I am the solution."

In Conclusion

If I may however, I would say this to everyone who reads it. If anyone you know talks about killing themselves, believe it and act appropriately. There are suicide prevention hot-lines in every city. I would advise you call and ask them what to do about your suicidal friend or family member. Don't laugh it off or dare them to go ahead. That is just plain stupid.

Contact: pjmcardle1@me.com

www.ingramcontent.com/pod-product-compliance
Lightning Source LLC
Chambersburg PA
CBHW050750180526
45159CB00003B/1410